Chemical Sector-Specific Plan

An Annex to the National Infrastructure Protection Plan

2010

Homeland
Security

Preface

The Chemical Sector-Specific Plan provides the unifying structure for the integration of Chemical Sector protection efforts into a single national program to help achieve the goal of a safe, secure, and resilient America through enhanced protection of the Nation's critical infrastructure and key resources (CIKR). As an annex to the National Infrastructure Protection Plan (NIPP), the Chemical Sector-Specific Plan describes how the NIPP risk management framework is being implemented in and integrated with both the voluntary programs already underway in the Chemical Sector and the promulgated regulatory standards for chemical facility security.

The Sector-Specific Plan represents a collaborative effort among the private sector; State, local, tribal, and territorial governments; nongovernmental organizations; and the Federal Government to mitigate the risk of our nation's critical infrastructure to all hazards, including terrorist attacks. Sector partners use the collaborative framework to prioritize protection initiatives and investments within and across sectors, decreasing the cost of regulatory compliance while minimizing the burden to industry. This process also ensures that resources are applied where they contribute the most to resilience and risk mitigation by lowering vulnerabilities, deterring threats, and minimizing the consequences of attacks and other incidents.

The 2010 release of the Chemical Sector-Specific Plan reflects the maturation of the Chemical Sector partnership and the progress of sector programs first outlined in the 2007 Sector-Specific Plan and subsequently expanded to address the needs and interests of sector partners. Examples of Chemical Sector accomplishments since publication of the 2007 Sector-Specific Plan include:

- Developing the Web-based Chemical Security Assessment Tool (CSAT), which allows DHS to collect chemical facility information in order to identify high-risk chemical facilities;

- Using the CSAT suite of tools to review over 38,000 consequence assessments submitted by chemical facilities since 2007, approximately 5,000 of which have been deemed high-risk chemical facilities subject to CFATS;[1]

- Spending over one million man hours on vulnerability assessments at high-risk facilities to determine where resources would be used most effectively on protection and resilience activities;

- Implementing private sector security guidance programs, documents, and plans at facilities nationwide, demonstrating the initiative taken by the owners, operators, and SCC member associations to improve security practices sector-wide;

- Hosting and participating in various outreach opportunities, including trade association conferences, event blogs, and Webinars that allow member companies to share Best Management Practices within the security arena;

---

[1] As of April 30, 2010.

- Hosting an annual Chemical Sector Security Summit since 2007, which provides an opportunity for chemical security professionals in the public and private sectors to exchange information and ideas regarding chemical security best practices and receive updates on security regulations;

- Developing and launching the Web-based Chemical Security Awareness Training Program to increase security awareness for all facility employees;

- Creating the free Web-based Voluntary Chemical Assessment Tool allowing owners and operators to assess risks and vulnerabilities and providing a cost-benefit analysis based on selected physical security countermeasures and mitigation strategies;

- Collaborating with State chemical industry councils to create the Security Exercise and Seminar Series, engaging facility owners and operators and their local emergency responders in an interactive seminar and tabletop planning exercise;

- Participating in National Level Exercises to test the efficiency of information-sharing mechanisms between public and private sector partners; and

- Developing a *Roadmap to Secure Control Systems in the Chemical Sector* and a corresponding implementation strategy to achieve the stated goals and milestones.

The risk mitigation activities summarized above were developed to align with the sector goals and objectives reported in the Chemical Sector-Specific Plan. Each year the Chemical Sector CIKR Protection Annual Report highlights the progress of these and other risk mitigation activities and summarizes the efforts of sector partners to identify, prioritize, and coordinate the protection of its critical infrastructure in accordance with the plans and strategies set out in the Sector-Specific Plan.

The Chemical Sector Coordinating Council and Government Coordinating Council are pleased to support the 2010 Chemical Sector-Specific Plan and look forward to strengthening the sector partnership to sustain and enhance the protection and resilience of critical infrastructure in the Chemical Sector.

Todd M. Keil	W. Craig Conklin	Dan Walters
Assistant Secretary for Infrastructure Protection U.S. Department of Homeland Security	Director, SSA Executive Management Office U.S. Department of Homeland Security Chair, Chemical GCC	Chair Chemical Sector Coordinating Council

Table of Contents

List of Figures

List of Tables

Executive Summary

The Chemical Sector is an integral component of the U.S. economy, converting various raw materials into more than 70,000 diverse products, many of which are critical to the health and well-being of the Nation's citizenry, security, and economy. Due to its size and business characteristics, the Chemical Sector may be an attractive target for attack. Moreover, many chemicals, either in their base form or when combined with others, can cause significant injuries if used maliciously. To help manage this risk, the U.S. Department of Homeland Security (DHS) and its security partners have developed the Chemical Sector-Specific Plan.

The Chemical Sector-Specific Plan provides the unifying structure for the integration of Chemical Sector protection efforts into a single national program to help achieve the goal of a safer, more secure America through enhanced protection of the Nation's critical infrastructure and key resources (CIKR). As an annex to the National Infrastructure Protection Plan (NIPP), the Chemical Sector-Specific Plan describes how the NIPP risk management framework is being implemented in and integrated with both the voluntary programs already underway in the Chemical Sector and the enacted chemical facility security regulatory standards.

1. Sector Profile and Goals

Several hundred thousand facilities in the United States in some manner use, manufacture, store, transport, or deliver chemicals, encompassing everything from petroleum refineries to pharmaceutical manufacturers to hardware stores. The facilities that make up the Chemical Sector typically belong to one of four key functional areas: (1) manufacturing plants, (2) transport systems, (3) warehousing and storage systems, and (4) chemical end users. While the key functional areas primarily describe their physical characteristics and activities, each of the four functional areas depends on cyber systems for a variety of purposes, including operating manufacturing processes, tracking inventory, and storing customer information.

A fundamental objective of the 2009 NIPP is to identify and take action to protect or improve the resilience of infrastructure identified as being critical. As one of the oldest industries in the country, the chemical industry has a long history of resilience based on the sector's ability to adapt to, prevent, prepare for, and recover from all hazards, including natural disasters, fluctuating markets, or a change in regulatory programs. To maintain operational resilience, successful businesses identify their critical dependencies and interdependencies and develop appropriate strategies to manage disruptions in critical systems should they occur.

The Chemical Sector also has a long and well-documented history of legislation and regulation addressing health, safety, accident prevention, emergency response, and the environment. In recent years, the U.S. Congress granted specific authority for regulations that focus on chemical security. While some of the legislation focuses on securing chemicals while in transit, perhaps the most critical for the sector is legislation that pertains to securing the most hazardous chemicals at a facility, namely the Maritime Transportation Security Act of 2002 (MTSA) and the Chemical Facility Anti-Terrorism Standards (CFATS).

Under MTSA, one of the regulatory authorities granted to DHS was the security of chemical facilities adjacent to navigable waters that may be involved in transportation security incidents. The authority to regulate security at the highest risk chemical facilities was granted to DHS in 2006. CFATS, the regulation implementing the authority, authorizes DHS to require high-risk chemical facilities to complete Security Vulnerability Assessments (SVAs), develop Site Security Plans, and implement the protective measures necessary to meet the Risk-Based Performance Standards (RBPS) established by DHS.

Sector Partners

In each CIKR sector, a variety of different entities in the private sector and all levels of government play key roles in securing the sectors. In the Chemical Sector, Federal partners engaged in chemical security are represented on the Chemical Government Coordinating Council (GCC), which is chaired by DHS. Partners include many different entities within DHS, as well as the U.S. Environmental Protection Agency (EPA), the Federal Bureau of Investigation (FBI), and the U.S. Department of Transportation (DOT), among others. State, local, tribal, and territorial governments also play a valuable role in Chemical Sector security and representatives from these groups are also members of the GCC.

As the owners of CIKR in the sector, private sector partners are critical to Chemical Sector protection and resilience. The major chemical industry trade associations represent owners and operators on the Chemical Sector Coordinating Council (SCC). In addition, owners and operators are nominated for both the chair and vice chair positions on the SCC.

Sector Goals

Over the past 3 years, partnerships in the Chemical Sector have matured along with the programs that have been implemented to strengthen the sector's protective posture. The goals and objectives, and the mission and vision statements in this document were revised and developed in collaboration with sector partners. These groups will continue to work together to implement activities in furtherance of the sector's strategic plan.

Goals for the Chemical Sector

Goal 1: Evaluate the security posture of Chemical Sector high-risk assets, including physical, cyber, and human elements as needed.

Goal 2: Prioritize Chemical Sector critical infrastructure protection activities based on risk.

Goal 3: Sustain risk-based, cost-effective sector-wide protective programs that increase asset-specific resilience without hindering the economic viability of the sector.

Goal 4: Refine processes and mechanisms for ongoing government/private sector coordination to increase sector resilience, as necessary.

Goal 5: Support risk-based critical infrastructure protection research and development (R&D) projects that add value to the Chemical Sector.

Goal 6: Measure the progress and effectiveness of sector critical infrastructure protection activities.

---

2. Identify Assets, Systems, and Networks

To effectively manage Chemical Sector protective efforts using a risk-based approach, DHS first needs to identify what assets, systems, and networks make up the sector. Information on Chemical Sector infrastructure, including physical, cyber, and human elements, is maintained by DHS in the Infrastructure Data Warehouse (IDW). The majority of Chemical Sector assets and infrastructure information are identified through regulatory programs, but are included in the IDW only to the extent allowable by the data protection programs developed in conjunction with the regulations.

In addition to identifying CIKR, DHS is responsible for prioritizing CIKR in all 18 sectors. DHS executes this responsibility through the National Critical Infrastructure Prioritization Program (NCIPP), which is intended to identify the Nation's most critical assets and systems that if disrupted could critically impact the public health and safety, economy, or national security. Within the Chemical Sector, most of these assets are identified through the CFATS and MTSA regulatory programs. Assets meeting the NCIPP criteria are considered for inclusion in the program.

Additionally, the sector is engaged in a collaborative effort to identify critical industrial control systems via a roadmap that addresses future cybersecurity issues, challenges, and goals. Although working toward implementation of this roadmap is voluntary, it does align with the CFATS methodology of risk-based performance standards for securing critical cyber assets.

3. Assess Risks

Managing and mitigating risk is the cornerstone of CIKR protection and resilience efforts under the NIPP. Within the Chemical Sector, many different methodologies have been and continue to be used by chemical facility owners and operators to assess the risks associated with their facilities. For several decades, facility owners and operators have been required by regulations to perform risk assessments of their facilities as they pertain to safety, process safety, and environmental issues. More recently, sector partners developed and are actively promoting vulnerability assessment methodologies to address the security threat.

The cornerstone of the DHS risk management framework adopts the risk management methodology that risk to an asset, system, or network is a function of the likely consequences of a successful attack, vulnerabilities to an attack, and the likelihood or threat of an attack. Because not all chemical facilities face the same level of potential risk, legislation was enacted to secure the highest risk chemical facilities. CFATS, as discussed in Section 1, follows a three-step process that is accessible to facility owners and operators through the Chemical Security Assessment Tool (CSAT). Initially, a facility possessing one or more chemicals of interest completes a Top-Screen that allows DHS to look at the potential consequences associated with an attack on the facility and determine whether or not those potential consequences are significant enough to warrant additional assessments. Only those facilities with significant potential consequences are preliminarily tiered and asked to perform the CSAT SVA. The SVA is a detailed consequence analysis and vulnerability assessment on those physical and cyber assets associated with each chemical of interest. The CSAT SVA informs the Department's final tiering of high-risk facilities.

MTSA is a second regulation requiring an assessment of security risk to the sector. Those facilities regulated by MTSA must assess the likely consequences of an attack and conduct a vulnerability assessment of their facility. The Facility Security Assessment (FSA) and the Facility Security Plan (FSP) must be submitted to the local Captain of the Port (COTP) for approval. In addition, the COTP and other port stakeholders utilize the Maritime Security Risk Assessment Model (MSRAM) to assess consequences and vulnerabilities at the port level. While MTSA facilities are not tiered, it is expected that the security posture of a chemical facility will be appropriate for the associated risk.

Threat is the last factor considered when assessing risk, but its determination is beyond the ability of many sector partners. Consequently, most asset owners and operators rely on threat input from DHS in order to accurately calculate the risk associated with a given asset. To assist in threat and risk determination, the Chemical Sector-Specific Agency (SSA) works with the DHS Homeland Infrastructure Threat and Risk Analysis Center (HITRAC) to prepare an unclassified threat assessment that can be used by sector partners to support risk assessments. Additionally, DHS shares threat information with members of the Chemical Sector through monthly unclassified suspicious activity conference calls and biannual classified threat briefings. While these forums do not directly feed the development of risk scores, they do provide insight to sector partners on the overall threat to the chemical industry and on potential suspicious activity of which chemical facilities, local law enforcement, and others should be aware.

4. Prioritize Infrastructure

It would be virtually impossible to protect every infrastructure or resource against all hazards. Therefore, the Nation's CIKR protective programs and resilience strategies strive to prioritize assets using a risk-based approach. Within the Chemical Sector, DHS relies on information gathered through the CFATS and MTSA regulatory programs to prioritize assets.

The CFATS regulatory regime uses the CSAT to collect facility data and assign those facilities that are deemed to be high risk to one of four tiers. In assigning tiers, DHS considers a variety of factors for each facility, including information about the public health and safety risk and mission critical aspects of a facility's products.

Those chemical facilities that interface with regulated vessels and pose a high risk of being involved in a transportation security incident are regulated under MTSA. There is no process required by the regulation to tier MTSA facilities, but it is expected that the security posture of a chemical facility will be appropriate for the associated risk.

Critical assets identified and prioritized through these regulatory regimes are the primary means through which critical assets are identified for inclusion in the NCIPP.

5. Develop and Implement Protective Programs and Resilience Strategies

The next step in managing sector risk is the development and implementation of protective programs and resilience strategies. Critical infrastructure protection and resilience in the Chemical Sector is composed of a variety of activities that apply pre-incident, during an incident, and post-incident. This range of activities is referred to as the Protective Spectrum, and includes prevention, protection, response, recovery, and preparedness activities, all of which help to increase the resilience of the sector. Protective programs and resilience strategies in the Chemical Sector are divided into regulatory, voluntary, and private sector programs. Each type of program addresses the issue of chemical security in a different way, but collectively these programs serve to mitigate the overall risk to the sector.

Determining the Need for Protective Programs and Resilience Strategies

Since the development of the Chemical Sector-Specific Plan in 2007, the sector has been working on developing a process to identify future, nonregulatory protective program needs. Currently, the SSA, in collaboration with the SCC, GCC, and other sector partners, compares the sector risk profile prepared by HITRAC with sector priorities, goals, objectives, and existing programs. This process identifies where protective measures may be most needed and what vulnerabilities, consequences, or threats may need to be addressed in the future.

Research into potential solutions begins once a program need has been identified. Sector partners are consulted regarding existing programs that might be available, but partners may also consult other sectors to leverage existing programs that may be optimized for Chemical Sector use. This has been especially true for cybersecurity awareness programs. As the SSA for the Information Technology Sector, the National Cyber Security Division (NCSD) collaborates with the Chemical SSA to provide programs to fill this identified gap.

Protective Program and Resilience Strategy Implementation

After the need for a program and its viability are determined, program objectives and content are developed in collaboration with sector partners and, in some cases, in consultation with additional subject-matter experts. The sector establishes a Critical Infrastructure Partnership Advisory Council (CIPAC) Working Group to ensure that the private sector is engaged in all phases of program development and implementation.

6. Measure Effectiveness

As a first step in measuring program effectiveness, the NIPP Measurement and Reporting Office (MRO) is requiring each of the 18 CIKR sectors to identify risk mitigation activities[1] (RMA) and select those activities that are key to mitigating risk in the sector. Metrics are then developed to measure the progress of the identified key RMAs.

The Chemical Sector identified key RMAs based on the following criteria:

- The scope of the potential impact, which includes the number of facilities impacted from a security perspective and the number of people or facilities likely to adopt an activity;
- A targeted focus on reducing the specific risks identified in the Chemical Sector Strategic Homeland Infrastructure Risk Assessment Profile;
- Facilitation of information sharing across the sector; and
- The raising of awareness of cybersecurity issues.

The key RMAs include regulatory, private sector, and voluntary programs and activities, and are reported annually in the Chemical Sector Annual Report. Each of these categories has a distinct process for metrics development and data collection.

The SSA will rely on the implementing agencies to provide data for key regulatory RMAs. These agencies are required to report progress to numerous entities, including the White House, Congress, and others as required. The SSA will work in collaboration with these agencies to integrate appropriate regulatory metrics into the sector metrics program.

The private sector has developed a set of metrics for private sector programs that capture the progress that owners and operators are making in mitigating sector risk in the following areas: risk assessment, security planning, emergency response planning, business continuity planning, and cybersecurity. The industry association members of the SCC will work with their member companies to collect and aggregate the requested data before reporting to DHS. Over time, the metrics will be evaluated and modified as necessary to accurately capture the risk mitigation activities of the private sector.

The SSA is the lead coordinator for the key voluntary RMAs, which are typically developed with information sharing as a central component of the program. The SSA, in cooperation with sector partners, will strive to assess key voluntary RMAs based on the following:

- The effectiveness of the information-sharing process, which is determined by whether or not all interested stakeholders are involved and whether or not the information that is shared is disseminated in a timely manner; and
- The quality of the information that is shared, which is determined by considering whether the information is useful in assisting facilities to reduce risk and increase resilience.

---

[1] A risk mitigation activity is defined by the NIPP MRO as a program, tool, initiative, project, major task, or some other undertaking that directly or indirectly leads to a reduction in risk.

---

7. CIKR Protection Research and Development

Science and technology offer considerable promise in helping to develop efficient and cost-effective ways of mapping potential consequences, identifying potential threats, assessing risk and vulnerabilities, and enhancing the protective posture of Chemical Sector infrastructure. The SSA is working closely with the SCC Research and Development (R&D) Working Group and other sector partners to establish a focused R&D portfolio that will enhance the security of the Chemical Sector and align with the six strategic CIKR protection goals for the Chemical Sector.

The Chemical Sector's research priorities include, but are not limited to, the following:

- Studying toxicity;
- Tracking toxic chemicals during transport;
- Mitigating chemical releases;
- Developing effective decontamination methods; and
- Reducing the explosive potential of certain chemicals.

With these priorities in mind, the SSA develops the Chemical Sector R&D portfolio by following the development and progress of existing DHS Science and Technology Directorate (S&T) projects that impact the sector, as well as identifying and submitting process capability gaps to the S&T Integrated Product Team (IPT) process. The S&T IPT process includes 13 capstone IPTs. The Chemical/Biological IPT contains the bulk of the R&D projects with a direct impact on the Chemical Sector. The mission of this IPT is to increase the Nation's preparedness against chemical and biological threats through improved threat awareness, advanced surveillance and detection, and protective countermeasures. Many Chemical Sector partners participate in the technical and review meetings for these projects, providing both data and expertise to the researchers.

The Chemical SSA monitors the progress of existing and new R&D initiatives included in the Chemical Sector R&D portfolio and reports to the SCC R&D Working Group and the GCC on the status of each individual project. Sector partners are also particularly interested in the intended use and associated limitations of the final customer products. Therefore, as appropriate for each project of interest to the sector, sector partners will also be involved in the development and review of the Technology Transition Agreement document detailing the conditions for transitioning the product to the customer.

8. Managing and Coordinating SSA Responsibilities

Pursuant to Homeland Security Presidential Directive 7 (HSPD-7), DHS is responsible for managing and coordinating Chemical Sector security activities. Within DHS, the Office of Infrastructure Protection (IP) is designated as the SSA for six of the 18 sectors, and the SSA Executive Management Office (EMO) is the Federal entity within IP that administers the SSAs. The Chemical SSA is able to benefit from SSA EMO management of activities that affect all SSAs within this office by maximizing the efficiencies such an organization can provide. These planning and integration activities include the following:

- Managing resources and budgets;
- Hiring personnel to support SSA activities and programs; and
- Managing cross-sector activities and documents.

Each SSA within the SSA EMO assumes primary responsibility for sector-specific activities such as the following:

- Developing needed or requested programs and activities in collaboration with sector partners;
- Coordinating information with sector partners;

- Collaborating with sector partners during National Level Exercises (NLEs) or during incidents; and

- Working with the sector to ensure that risk assessment tools are under development or available for sector use.

The SSA is also responsible for fostering public-private partnerships so that all documents, programs, and activities are developed through a collaborative and iterative process. The SSA achieves this through regular interactions with the SCC and the GCC. The SCC coordinates Chemical Sector CIKR protection efforts with the private sector. The GCC acts as the organizing mechanism through which the SSA coordinates sector CIKR protection activities across the Federal Government, as well as with State, local, tribal, and territorial governments.

The triennial revision of the 2010 Chemical Sector-Specific Plan was developed through the successful partnership and working relationships that exist between the SSA and the SCC and GCC. This document describes the programs, activities, and processes that sector partners agree will guide the sector over the next three years.

Introduction

Protecting and ensuring the resilience of the critical infrastructure and key resources (CIKR) of the United States is essential to the Nation's security, public health and safety, economic vitality, and way of life. The responsibility for securing the Nation's CIKR is shared among Federal, State, local, tribal, and territorial governments and the private sector. The National Infrastructure Protection Plan (NIPP) was developed to coordinate the implementation of national CIKR protection and resilience efforts. The NIPP provides the unifying structure for the integration of existing and future CIKR protection efforts and resilience strategies into a single national program to achieve the goal of a safer, more secure, and more resilient America.

The NIPP is centered on a risk management framework that describes the processes for achieving the following:

- Setting goals and objectives;
- Identifying assets, systems, and networks;
- Assessing risks (consequences, vulnerabilities, and threats);
- Prioritizing CIKR;
- Implementing protective programs and resilience strategies; and
- Measuring the effectiveness of CIKR protection and resilience efforts.

As Figure I-1 indicates, the physical, cyber, and human elements of the infrastructure must be considered when implementing the framework.

Figure I-1: NIPP Risk Management Framework

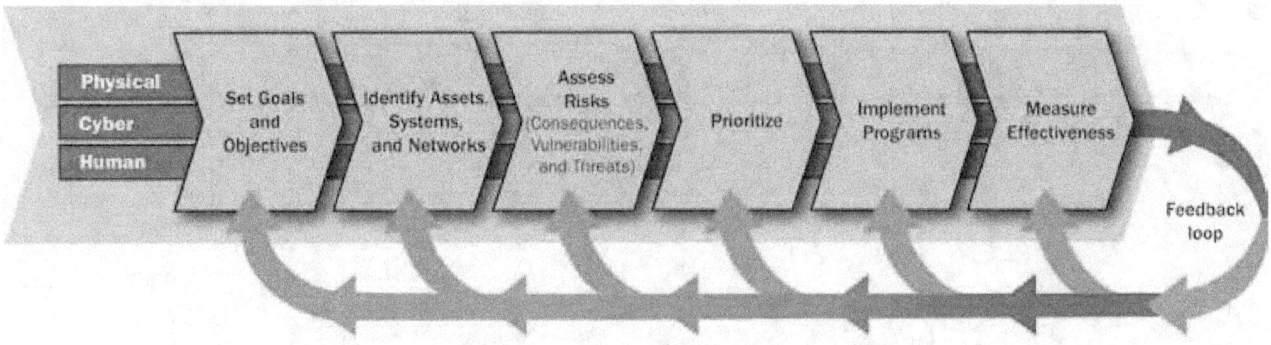

Continuous improvement to enhance protection of CIKR

In recognition of the unique characteristics associated with different assets, systems, and networks, the national infrastructure is divided into 18 distinct CIKR sectors. Federal agencies, designated as Sector-Specific Agencies (SSA), have been assigned to coordinate CIKR protection and resilience efforts in each of the sectors. The U.S. Department of Homeland Security (DHS) is designated as the SSA for the Chemical Sector.

As required by the NIPP, the SSA is responsible for coordinating the development of a Sector-Specific Plan that follows and supports the NIPP risk management framework, defines the roles and responsibilities of sector partners, outlines a research and development (R&D) plan for the sector, and describes how the SSA manages and coordinates its responsibilities.

The collaborative partnership, as outlined in the NIPP, allows sector partners to leverage existing practices and build on initiatives already developed by the private sector. Processes have been established in collaboration with sector partners to develop programs that promote the following:

• Information sharing among sector partners;

• Security training and awareness initiatives; and

• Education and outreach to sector partners.

Sector partners have been especially active in raising the awareness of cybersecurity issues. In addition to meeting regularly with several branches of the National Cyber Security Division (NCSD), sector partners are promoting vulnerability assessment tools for industrial control systems and business systems to make them less vulnerable to cyber attacks.

In addition to chemical security regulations enacted through the Maritime Transportation Security Act of 2002 (MTSA), DHS was granted authority over high-risk chemical facilities through implementation of the Chemical Facility Anti-Terrorism Standards (CFATS). This has significantly increased the security posture of the sector since the publication of the first Chemical Sector-Specific Plan in 2007. CFATS grants DHS the authority to require high-risk chemical facilities to complete vulnerability assessments, develop site security plans, and implement the protective measures necessary to meet DHS-defined performance standards. More than 5,000 high-risk chemical facilities have submitted security vulnerability assessments (SVAs) to DHS for review and have either submitted or are currently developing site security plans for submission to DHS.[2] In 2010, DHS will begin performing compliance inspections at these high-risk chemical facilities to ensure that proper site security plans are being implemented. In addition to regulating chemical security at facilities, legislation has also been enacted to reduce the security risk of chemicals during transport.

This document reflects the maturation of the public-private partnership in the Chemical Sector. Sector partners at all levels of government and the private sector were given the opportunity and were encouraged to comment on previous drafts. The Chemical SSA and members of the Chemical Sector Coordinating Council (SCC) met regularly throughout this process to ensure that both public and private sector perspectives were included.

Finally, the Chemical SSA welcomes inquiries on any of the material presented in this document. Please send questions and comments to **ChemicalSector@dhs.gov**.

---

[2] As of April 30, 2010. Note: Facilities completing an SVA are preliminarily determined to be high-risk.

1. Sector Profile and Goals

The Chemical Sector and the products that the sector produces are essential to many facets of modern life, including a safe water supply, energy production, increased food production, housing, healthcare, computer technology, and transportation (for additional information see Appendix 3). Our national and economic security, as well as our present standard of living, depends on the vitality of the Chemical Sector and the continued production and transportation of chemicals.

The sector has a well-developed and successful best practices approach to risk management with regard to safety issues. According to the U.S. Department of Labor, the chemical industry has one of the best safety records of all U.S. manufacturers.[3] After the September 11th attacks, many chemical companies leveraged this risk management approach to safety and applied it to the new security threat. The industry initiated a variety of voluntary security programs and made significant capital investments to address security concerns. Several States also adopted measures to enhance the security of the chemical facilities under their jurisdiction.

While acknowledging industry and State efforts to secure chemical facilities, the Federal Government continues to implement security regulations at sites that it deems to be at high risk to ensure a uniform approach to security. In addition, regulations have been passed to increase the security of chemicals during transport and distribution, including at the Nation's port facilities.

This chapter of the Chemical Sector-Specific Plan describes the nature and complexity of the Chemical Sector, of which a basic understanding is necessary for the coordination of critical infrastructure protection activities. Included is a profile of the sector that provides descriptions of the ways in which sector assets are classified; descriptions of the major public and private sector critical infrastructure and key resources (CIKR) partners and their relationship with DHS; the sector's regulatory environment; and an outline of the sector's mission, vision, goals, and objectives.

1.1 Sector Profile

The chemical industry is diverse, involving a variety of products and materials, and encompassing a wide variety of different functional activities. Typically, Chemical Sector infrastructure is classified by functional area within the industry supply chain.

The chemical industry supply chain encompasses activities associated with the procurement of raw materials and with the design, manufacture, marketing, distribution, transport, customer support, use, recycling, and disposal of chemical products. By examining the supply chain and the services that support it, Chemical Sector infrastructure can be divided into four key

---

[3] National Infrastructure Advisory Council, *Chemical, Biological, and Radiological Events, and the Critical Infrastructure Workforce: Final Report and Recommendations*, January 2008, p. 29, **http://www.dhs.gov/xlibrary/assets/niac/niac_CBR_FINAL_REPORT.pdf**.

functional areas: (1) manufacturing plants; (2) transport systems; (3) warehousing and storage systems, including stockpile and supply areas; and (4) chemical end users. While the descriptions of these key functional areas are primarily centered on their physical characteristics and activities, each of the four functional areas depends on cyber systems for a variety of purposes, including the following:

- Operating manufacturing processes using automated industrial control systems and process safety systems;

- Tracking inventory, storage, and movement of chemical products;

- Storing customer information, including products that are bought on a regular basis and the locations where they are typically sent;

- Storing personnel information to prevent the theft of personal identity information; and

- Operating perimeter security systems.

Personnel surety is also an important aspect of securing cyber systems at chemical facilities. Many companies in the sector have mitigated the risk of coercion or insider threat by utilizing policies, practices, and technologies that protect the linkage of critical plant systems with corporate networks. Secure authentication technology may be used to restrict access based on roles and clearances while proper policies are employed to terminate user accounts once an employee's relationship with the company is terminated.

As a result of the importance of cyber systems in the sector and the focused effort on cybersecurity, many companies are trying to improve communication among industrial control systems security, the security of business systems, and physical security. Companies are increasingly likely to include an information technology security representative on the corporate crisis management team. Other members of the crisis management team may include representatives from the public affairs office, physical security officers, and representatives from business and finance.

1.1.1 Manufacturing Plants

Manufacturing plants convert raw materials (upstream components) into intermediate and end products (downstream components). The sector has divided the chemical manufacturing process into five stages, each of which may contain one or more processing activities:

1. Receipt of chemical ingredients;

2. Temporary staging or storing of chemical ingredients awaiting use in production;

3. Processing of chemical ingredients into products or intermediates;

4. Temporary staging or storing of chemical products awaiting shipment; and

5. Staging for shipping chemical products.

A modern chemical manufacturing facility is highly automated and complex. The design, construction, and operation of these facilities require a diverse range of expertise to address safety, health, environmental, and security concerns. The automation of processes has become integral as well. Industrial automated systems, including process safety systems, can be connected to a larger company computer network system that may have controlled remote access. The security of these systems is essential to ensure that chemicals and products are tracked, accounted for, and routed appropriately once staged and shipped out of facilities.

1.1.2 Transport Systems

Given both the location of production plants relative to consumers and the hazardous nature of many of the materials used throughout the chemical manufacturing process, transport of materials has become a distinct functional area, with many safety and security requirements of its own. Included in the transportation functional area of the Chemical Sector are the means for providing raw materials to the manufacturing plants, transporting intermediate products both within and among chemical facilities, and distributing products to end users. The transportation of chemicals involves intrastate, interstate, and foreign commerce. The sector uses all modes of transportation—rail, highway, maritime, air, and pipeline. Multiple sizes and configurations of packaging are used to transport chemicals, including bulk packaging such as tank cars and cargo tanks, and nonbulk packaging such as bags, drums, and boxes.

Companies and facilities involved with chemical transport use a combination of manual and automated systems to control customer order placement and transportation, including remote location detection systems and systems to secure shipment details and customer information.

1.1.3 Warehousing and Storage Systems

Chemical warehousing and storage systems primarily provide two important operational functions: (1) downsized repackaging, and (2) storage. Combined, these activities ensure that the proper quantities of chemicals are efficiently situated for cost-effective and timely delivery to customers across the country. As with upstream manufacturing, automation through the use of cyber systems is vital at many of these facilities to ensure accurate inventory, timely receipt and shipment of chemicals, and onsite and remote monitoring of the facilities. Chemicals shipped through warehousing and storage systems are used by customers to produce a variety of products, including food flavorings, perfumes, water purifiers, computers, plastics, paints and coatings, textiles, cosmetics and toiletries, detergents, automobile parts, rubber compounds, fiberglass, and pharmaceuticals.

Warehousing and storage is an essential support function in the production process. The availability of warehousing and storage facilities supports a steady flow of raw materials and consumer goods. The adequacy of storage and logistics infrastructure can have a strong influence on the prices paid by consumers.

Warehousing facilities typically store bulk chemicals in fixed tanks, while other chemicals may be stored in tank cars, cargo tanks, and barges for short durations. Chemical facilities also store products in smaller packages, such as drums, cylinders, and pails. Additionally, chemical storage may occur at a variety of end-user facilities, such as water treatment facilities, petroleum refineries, and at other downstream manufacturers and consumers of chemicals.

1.1.4 Chemical End Users

The final stage of the chemical industry supply chain encompasses a number of end users from a variety of businesses, including food services, agriculture, healthcare, mining, science and technology, and education. The chemicals are used for many purposes, such as sanitizers, refrigerants, fertilizers, explosives, paints, pharmaceutical products, and for high-tech R&D. Typically, end users consume the chemicals that they purchase.

1.1.5 Scope and Size of the Sector

While the task of broadly defining the sector is relatively easy, defining the sector in terms of the number of sites or facilities is much more challenging. As the SSA for the Chemical Sector, DHS is responsible for managing and coordinating CIKR protection activities and resilience strategies with the sector. Maintaining a database of chemical facilities enhances the ability of the SSA to develop effective protection programs and resilience strategies with the sector.

DHS estimates that 50,000 or more facilities throughout the Nation may possess sufficient quantities of chemicals of interest requiring the facilities to submit information to DHS. This information would allow DHS to assess their potential security risk under the Chemical Facilities Anti-Terrorism Standards (CFATS). More than 38,000 such sites have submitted information to DHS under CFATS.[4] DHS is working with the States and other CIKR partners on programs to identify additional facilities that may need to complete this assessment.

The SSA is committed to working with all sites that store or use chemicals in order to provide the tools and support necessary to better prepare these facilities for both natural disasters and a deliberate attack. To better define the full range of chemical sites, the SSA is collaborating with the States to develop a database of sites across the Nation that must comply with the Superfund Amendments and Reauthorization Act (SARA) Title III reporting requirements. Facilities that have chemicals subject to the Occupational Safety and Health Administration's (OSHA's) Hazard Communication Standard (29 CFR 1919.1200) at reporting thresholds set by the Environmental Protection Agency in 40 CFR 370 must provide a hazardous chemical inventory form annually to their State Emergency Response Commission (SERC), Local Emergency Planning Committee (LEPC), and their local fire department. The Chemical SSA is working with States to collect and store this information in a DHS-administered database known as the Chemical and Hazardous Information Reference Portal (CHIRP). Data collection efforts are still in progress, but it is expected that the number of sites in the database will be significantly larger than the number of regulated sites due to the large number of qualifying chemical products and the lower threshold quantities that trigger the reporting requirements.

1.1.6 Resilience in the Sector

A fundamental objective of the NIPP is to identify and take action to protect or improve the resilience of infrastructure identified as "critical." The NIPP defines resilience as "the ability to resist, absorb, recover from, or successfully adapt to adversity or a change in conditions" (NIPP, 2009, p. 111). As one of the oldest industries in the country, the chemical industry has a long history of resilience based on the sector's ability to adapt to, prevent, prepare for, and recover from all hazards.[5]

A key element of prevention and preparation is an emergency response plan. Emergency response plans are prevalent in the Chemical Sector and are also often required as part of CFATS, the Maritime Transportation Security Act (MTSA), the Environmental Protection Agency's (EPA) Risk Management Program (RMP), the Resource Conservation and Recovery Act (RCRA), and OSHA regulations. These plans are typically coordinated with the local community emergency response plans and follow the National Incident Management System (NIMS). In addition, the sector will have a preparedness alternative to utilize when the DHS Voluntary Private Sector Accreditation and Certification Preparedness program is implemented as required by the Implementing the Recommendations of the 9/11 Commission Act of 2007.[6]

Successful businesses in the sector adjust to changing conditions, whether the source of the change is a natural disaster, fluctuating markets, or a change in the regulatory programs that require careful management, storage, use, disposal, and clean-up of chemicals. The Chemical Sector recognizes that resilient operations and effective loss prevention are a part of managing risk. In today's business environment, a business continuity plan is at the center of a business's ability to successfully adapt to changing conditions. A successful plan will identify critical interdependencies and determine the length of time that it is possible to operate without critical systems before undesirable losses occur, as well as identify implementation strategies to prevent those undesirable losses.

The SSA recognizes that a significant number of businesses within the sector have procedures in place that help them improve resilience. The SSA is working with businesses and industry associations to determine gaps where the SSA can facilitate efforts to increase resilience in the sector, as well as across sectors that are dependent on or interdependent with the Chemical Sector.

---

[4] As of April 30, 2010.

[5] As defined in the 2009 NIPP, all hazards encompass all conditions, environmental or manmade, that have the potential to cause injury, illness, or death; damage to or loss of equipment, infrastructure services, or property; or alternatively cause functional degradation to social, economic, or environmental aspects.

[6] While the Chemical Sector Coordinating Council has reservations about this program, they have agreed to work with DHS to leverage existing preparedness initiatives already being used by industry in the sector. Some of these initiatives are listed in Appendix 8.

For example, the SSA is keeping sector partners engaged in a DHS effort to develop modeling and simulation methods to determine the resilience of the sector when an event or incident occurs.

1.1.7 Interdependencies and Overlapping Relationships With Other CIKR Sectors

Many assets, systems, and networks are dependent on elements of other assets, systems, and networks to maintain functionality. In some cases, a failure in one sector will have a significant impact on the ability of another sector to perform necessary functions. Reliance on another sector for functionality is called a dependency (see Figure 1-1). If two pieces of infrastructure are dependent on one another, then they are interdependent. It is extremely important to identify dependencies and interdependencies, both at the sector level as well as the asset, system, or network level, in order to fully understand the consequences of a disruption or attack on a piece of infrastructure. This information also helps identify the manner in which disruptions or attacks on other infrastructure could impact an interdependent asset, system, or network.

Figure 1-1: Chemical Sector Dependencies and Interdependencies

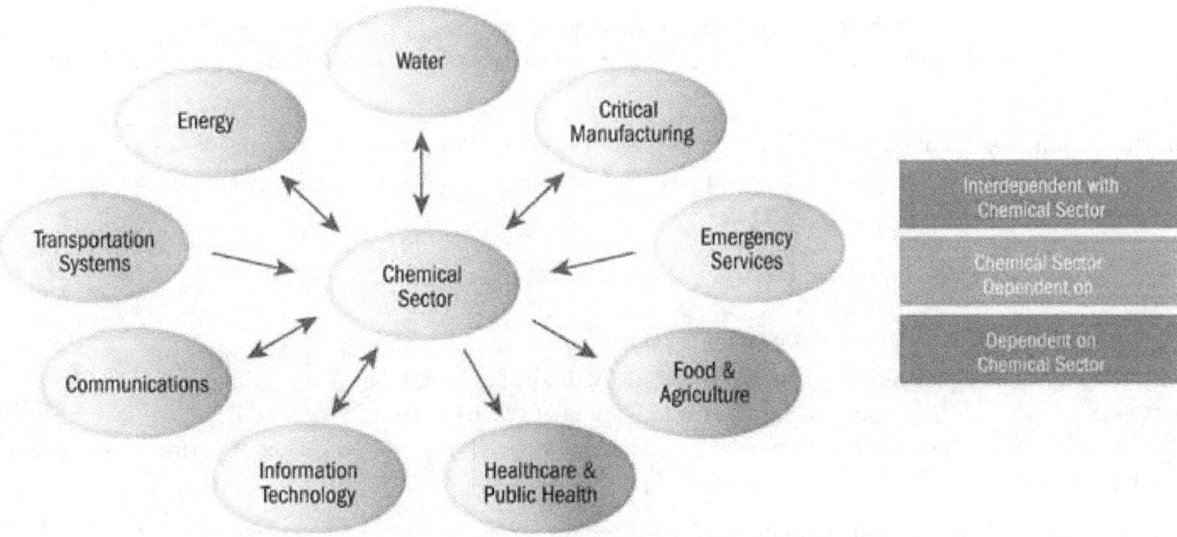

The Chemical Sector is dependent on many other sectors to maintain full functionality. For instance, technology solutions from the Information Technology (IT) and Communications Sectors play a vital role in supporting performance, operation, and communication through all aspects of the chemical industry supply chain. The sector is also highly dependent on rail, trucking, and pipeline services for the secure transport of its products to customers who need them. Conversely, many industries are reliant on the Chemical Sector. For example, chlorine is critical in pharmaceutical production as well as the purification of drinking water, and explosives are essential to mine coal for energy production. In addition, pesticides, fertilizers, and preservatives help ensure a safe and abundant food supply.

The Chemical Sector also overlaps with various other CIKR sectors. For instance, pharmaceutical manufacturers can be considered both a part of the Chemical Sector and the Healthcare and Public Health Sector. Similarly, petrochemical refineries are part of both the Chemical and Energy Sectors. More information on the CIKR sectors that depend on, are depended on by, or overlap with the Chemical Sector can be found in Appendix 4.

In order to assess international dependencies and interdependencies, DHS implemented the Critical Foreign Dependencies Initiative (CFDI). Developed in close collaboration with the U.S. Department of State (DOS), as well as other partners in the critical infrastructure protection and intelligence communities, CFDI helps identify assets and systems outside the United States that are critical to the Nation's public health, economic security, or national security. The SSA will continue to participate in this program and work with partners to identify any critical foreign infrastructure in the future.

1.1.8 Sector Regulatory Profile

The Chemical Sector's history regarding legislation and regulations addressing health, safety, accident prevention, emergency response, and the environment is well documented. In recent years, Congress granted specific authority for regulations that focus on chemical security. Chemical security legislation addresses the collection of asset-specific information, requires vulnerability assessments, promotes information sharing while ensuring the protection of the information, and encourages or requires identification of protective strategies and implementation of protective programs. While most of the legislation pertains to securing the most hazardous chemicals at a facility, some legislation focuses on securing these chemicals while in transit.

Industry association members of the Chemical SCC have collectively or individually submitted comments on proposed rules to ensure that pertinent information is shared with the regulatory authority and that the private sector perspective is captured. In addition, to inform the development of regulations, private sector partners have hosted site visits to chemical facilities for public sector partners.

The following security regulations significantly impact the security of the sector and are listed by the department having the authority to implement the legislation. A more complete listing of existing authorities and regulations is contained in Appendix 5.

1.1.8.1 U.S. Department of Homeland Security

1.1.8.1.1 Chemical Facility Anti-Terrorism Standards

Section 550 of the DHS Appropriations Act of 2007 gave DHS the authority to regulate the security of high-risk chemical facilities.[7] CFATS authorizes DHS to require high-risk chemical facilities to complete Security Vulnerability Assessments (SVAs), develop Site Security Plans, and implement the protective measures necessary to meet the Risk-Based Performance Standards (RBPS) established by DHS.

To help identify potential high-risk chemical facilities subject to regulation under CFATS, DHS developed a list of chemicals that, if possessed above certain threshold quantities by a facility, require the facility to complete and submit to DHS a Top-Screen assessment, which will allow DHS to preliminarily assess a facility's security risk. This list is contained in Appendix A to CFATS. Approximately 300 chemicals that have the potential to create significant human health impacts if released, stolen, diverted, or sabotaged are listed as chemicals of interest (COI) in Appendix A. Generally speaking, if a facility possesses any COI in an amount equal to or greater than the corresponding Screening Threshold Quantity (STQ), it must complete and submit to the Department an online questionnaire (the Chemical Security Assessment Tool (CSAT) Top-Screen), which will provide the Department with additional information from which it can determine preliminarily if a facility is a high-risk chemical facility.

If DHS determines upon review of a Top-Screen that a facility is high risk, DHS will issue a preliminary tiering and the facility is then required to complete and submit to DHS an SVA or, for certain lower risk facilities, an alternate security program (ASP) in lieu of an SVA. DHS will review the SVA or ASP and determine whether or not a facility is, in fact, high risk. Facilities that are determined to be high risk at this point will receive a final tiering from DHS, and are required to submit a Site Security Plan or

---

[7] Facilities regulated under MTSA or by the Nuclear Regulatory Commission (NRC), facilities owned or operated by the U.S. Department of Defense (DOD) or the U.S. Department of Energy (DOE), public water systems (as defined by Section 1401 of the Safe Drinking Water Act), and water treatment works (as defined by Section 212 of the Federal Water Pollution Control Act) are currently statutorily exempt from regulation under Section 550. However, in Fall 2009, discussions were held in Congress to reexamine the exemptions.

ASP. A Site Security Plan or ASP will detail the specific security measures that a facility has implemented or will implement to meet the RBPS established by DHS. Facilities have flexibility in determining what security measures or processes to implement to meet the CFATS RBPS, and DHS expects facilities to implement measures and processes that are appropriate given the facility's risk tier, security issues, and other relevant factors. DHS will review the Site Security Plans or ASPs and conduct periodic on-site facility inspections to ensure compliance with the submitted plan.

Congress recently extended the Department's CFATS authority through October 2010, and is currently evaluating approaches for making the CFATS program permanent.[8]

1.1.8.1.2 Maritime Transportation Security Act of 2002

Under MTSA (46 United States Code (U.S.C.) 70101 et seq.), the United States Coast Guard (USCG) regulates commercial maritime transportation of bulk and packaged chemicals, as well as the security of chemical facilities adjacent to navigable waters that may be involved in transportation security incidents. This authority includes the collection and maintenance of essential infrastructure information concerning these facilities, as well as review and approval of facility security assessments (FSAs) and facility security plans (FSPs).

Under MTSA, the USCG established area maritime security committees and prepared area maritime security plans, which require assessments of ports, vessels, and U.S. facilities in order to identify those that pose a high risk of being involved in a transportation security incident. Additionally, MTSA requires owners and operators of chemical facilities located contiguous to waterways to complete FSAs and submit FSPs to the USCG for review and approval. Approximately 400 chemical facilities are subject to these requirements. FSPs must include security measures; procedures for responding to security threats; and detailed preparedness, prevention, and response activities for each maritime security (MARSEC) level. High-risk vessels must also submit security assessments and security plans. The USCG also ensures that foreign flag vessels meet certain security standards.

Transportation Worker Identification Credential

Transportation Worker Identification Credentials (TWICs) are tamper-resistant biometric credentials issued to workers who require unescorted access to secure areas of MTSA-regulated ports, vessels, outer continental shelf facilities, and all credentialed merchant mariners. To obtain a TWIC, an individual must provide biographic and biometric information such as fingerprints, sit for a digital photograph, and successfully pass a security threat assessment conducted by the Transportation Security Administration (TSA). TWIC was developed in accordance with the legislative provisions of MTSA and the Security and Accountability for Every (SAFE) Port Act. The USCG is responsible for enforcement of the TWIC regulations in the maritime domain.

All workers who require unescorted access to secure areas of maritime facilities and vessels, as well as all U.S.-credentialed mariners, should have been in compliance by April 15, 2009.

Transportation Worker Identification Credential—Reader Requirements has been released for Advance Notice of Proposed Rulemaking. The public comment period for the proposed rule ended May 26, 2009. The rule will provide guidance on the frequency of biometric checks against TWIC stored data. Frequency will be based on the risk posed by the facility as defined by the USCG.

---

[8] To this end, on November 6, 2009, the U.S. House of Representatives passed H.R. 2868, which would expand DHS's chemical facility security regulatory authority. H.R. 2868 includes language to address a citizen petition process, protection of information, whistleblower protections, employee background checks at tiered facilities, and methods to reduce the consequences of a terrorist attack by assessing inherently safer technology (IST). The U.S. Senate will be considering similar legislation in 2010.

Private sector partners are concerned about the IST provision because IST is poorly understood by the general public. IST is a conceptual framework used by scientists and engineers to encompass chemical processing procedures, equipment, protection, and, when feasible, the use of safer substances. The private sector believes that IST is often misunderstood to refer only to reducing the amount of hazardous chemicals used in manufacturing and processing. However, a simple reduction in the use of hazardous chemicals is often not possible or may only result in the redistribution or transfer of risk, without actually reducing risk.

1.1.8.1.3 Rail Transportation Security

TSA published a final rule on November 26, 2008, that establishes security requirements for rail transportation, which covers freight railroad carriers and rail operations at certain, fixed-site facilities that ship or receive specified hazardous materials (HAZMAT) by rail, known as rail security-sensitive materials (RSSM) (49 CFR 1580.100 (b)). The rule codifies the scope of TSA's existing inspection program that requires regulated parties to allow TSA and other DHS officials to enter, inspect, and test property, facilities, and records relevant to rail security. This rule also requires parties to designate rail security coordinators and report significant security concerns to DHS. Freight rail carriers and certain facilities handling RSSM must have procedures in place to report location and shipping information to TSA upon request and within a specific time frame. Regulated entities must also implement chain-of-custody requirements to ensure a positive and secure exchange of RSSM. TSA also proposed to clarify and extend the sensitive security information (SSI) protections to cover certain information associated with rail transportation.

1.1.8.1.4 Secure Handling of Ammonium Nitrate

In the Fiscal Year (FY) 2008 Omnibus Appropriations Act, Congress amended the Homeland Security Act of 2002 (6 U.S.C. 361 et seq.) by adding Subtitle J, Secure Handling of Ammonium Nitrate (AN). Subtitle J authorizes DHS to regulate the sale and transfer of AN and requires that DHS develop a regulatory program that oversees or requires (1) the registration of AN sellers and AN purchasers with DHS, (2) point-of-sale verification of AN purchasers, (3) recordkeeping requirements for AN sales or transfers, (4) reporting requirements in cases of theft or loss, (5) compliance inspections, (6) guidance materials and informational posters for the benefit of both AN sellers and AN purchasers, and (7) appeals processes. Subtitle J also provides DHS with the authority to levy civil penalties of up to $50,000 per violation of the subsequent regulation.

DHS intends to release for public review and comment a Notice of Proposed Rulemaking containing a proposed rule for implementing Subtitle J in 2010.

1.1.8.2 U.S. Department of Transportation

1.1.8.2.1 Enhancing Rail Transportation Safety and Security for Hazardous Materials Shipments Rule

On November 26, 2008, the Pipeline and Hazardous Materials Safety Administration (PHMSA), in coordination with the Federal Railroad Administration and TSA, issued a final rule revising the current requirements in the HAZMAT regulations applicable to the safe and secure transportation of HAZMAT transported in commerce by rail. This rule fulfills requirements in Section 1551 of the Implementing Recommendations of the 9/11 Commission Act of 2007 (Public Law 110-53, August 3, 2007). Rail carriers are required to compile annual data on certain shipments of explosive, toxic by inhalation, and radioactive materials. This data will be used to analyze safety and security risks along rail routes where those materials are transported, assess alternative routing options, and make routing decisions based on those assessments. The rule also clarifies rail carriers' responsibility to address in their security plans issues related to en route storage and delays in transit. In addition, a new requirement was adopted for rail carriers to inspect placarded HAZMAT rail cars for signs of tampering or suspicious items, including improvised explosive devices.

1.1.8.2.2 Hazardous Materials Transportation Act

Under the Hazardous Materials Transportation Act (49 U.S.C. 5101 et seq.), the U.S. Department of Transportation (DOT) has the authority to promulgate regulations regarding the safe and secure shipment of HAZMAT. Within DOT, this responsibility has been delegated to PHMSA with enforcement authority shared by the modal administrations. Pursuant to this authority, PHMSA has established regulations governing the transportation of HAZMAT on public highways, by rail, in aircraft, and in vessels. In general, commercial HAZMAT move by permission of DOT granted through compliance with PHMSA's regulations, which are internationally harmonized to ensure that transportation is not unduly impeded. These regulations cover classification, packaging, emergency communication, training, and modal-specific requirements. Among PHMSA's rules are those that require sellers and transporters of certain types of HAZMAT to develop and implement security plans and conduct security training for employees. Security plans must be based on vulnerability assessments and must address personnel, access, and en route security related to HAZMAT in transportation. PHMSA ensures that the Nation's HAZMAT transportation rules are uniform through its preemptive authority over non-Federal requirements. PHMSA serves as the U.S. authority for HAZMAT transportation safety and security in international forums.

The Federal Motor Carrier Safety Administration (FMCSA) has also been delegated several authorities under the Hazardous Materials Transportation Act. These include the operational aspects of the vehicles used to carry HAZMAT. In addition to routing and safety permits, FMCSA rules prohibit States from issuing, renewing, transferring, or upgrading a commercial driver's license with a HAZMAT endorsement unless the TSA has first conducted a fingerprint-based records assessment of the applicant and determined that the applicant does not pose a security risk warranting denial of the HAZMAT endorsement (49 CFR Parts 383 and 384). The FMCSA also requires States to establish a HAZMAT endorsement renewal period of no more than five years to ensure that each holder of a HAZMAT endorsement routinely and uniformly receives a security screening.

1.1.8.3 State and Local Authorities

Before the Federal Government regulated chemical facility security, several State and local laws and authorities were proposed or enacted that addressed security at chemical facilities located or operating within State and local jurisdictions. Most of these authorities included activities such as conducting vulnerability assessments and implementing appropriate security measures. In addition, the State of New Jersey also required the consideration of inherently safer technology as a component of a facility's security plan. The issue of review and preemption of State laws and regulations as they pertain to chemical security is discussed in 6 CFR 27.405. A list of the significant State and local authorities directed at increasing security at chemical facilities is included in Appendix 5.

Through the State, Local, Tribal, and Territorial Government Coordinating Council (SLTTGCC), DHS continues to engage State representatives and maintains particularly focused dialogue with States regulating the security of chemical facilities in their jurisdiction.

1.1.8.4 Harmonization of Security Regulations

Since the publication of the first Chemical Sector-Specific Plan in 2007, the number of security-related regulations impacting the sector has increased. Owners and operators in the Chemical Sector identified the lack of harmonization among the different regulatory authorities as a challenge. Facilities that are covered by more than one authority often face multiple requirements and compliance inspections. This has the potential to create a number of conflicting requirements that, if unresolved, could slow implementation of security measures or undermine security at impacted facilities.

Government regulators are engaged in significant efforts to harmonize regulatory programs where appropriate. In particular, the DHS division responsible for implementing CFATS and the Secure Handling of Ammonium Nitrate regulations—the Office of Infrastructure Protection's (IP) Infrastructure Security Compliance Division (ISCD)—is collaborating with various other Federal entities to minimize duplication of efforts and to ensure efficient use of government and private sector resources, all while closing any security gaps that may exist within the Chemical Sector. These efforts include the following:

- The establishment of an ISCD/USCG Working Group whose mission is to harmonize CFATS and MTSA regulations. This working group is developing an intra-agency agreement that will outline the parameters of ISCD/USCG coordination under CFATS and MTSA, as well as standard operating procedures that will allow ISCD and USCG to identify facilities subject to both regulations, clearly delineate the lines of jurisdictional authority for those sites that are subject to both CFATS and MTSA, and inform how inspections will occur at those facilities. In addition, these agencies are also investigating ways to harmonize performance criteria under the two regulations to ensure that security expectations for chemical facilities that pose the same level of risk are consistent under the two regulations.

- ISCD is working on a Memorandum of Agreement (MOA) with the Nuclear Regulatory Commission (NRC) establishing the manner in which the NRC and ISCD intend to determine if a facility is wholly or partially exempt from CFATS pursuant to the NRC exemption contained in Section 550. Concurrently, ISCD and NRC are engaging in joint visits of NRC-regulated facilities to review how chemicals of interest are currently secured at such facilities with the ultimate goal of ensuring that such chemicals are properly secured regardless of which agency has jurisdiction over the portion of the facility where the chemicals are located.

- ISCD is working closely with TSA to ensure that CFATS and the Rail Transportation Security Regulations (RTSR) are complementary to each other and to eliminate security gaps that may exist as chemicals move through the value chain. This includes efforts to determine the potential application of the RBPS to the Rail Secure Areas regulated under the RTSR.

- ISCD is in the initial stages of development of an MOA with the Federal Bureau of Investigation (FBI) regarding chemical facility security. Such an MOA would help formalize the current information-sharing and collaboration activities already taking place between the two agencies regarding chemical facility security.

- ISCD has been working with the FBI and the Bureau of Alcohol, Tobacco, Firearms, and Explosives (ATF) during the development of regulations to implement the Secure Handling of Ammonium Nitrate. ISCD and ATF are working especially closely to ensure that the final version of the Secure Handling of Ammonium Nitrate regulations and the Federal Explosives Laws, both of which regulate certain AN mixtures, are complementary and not duplicative.

1.2 CIKR Partners

There are a wide variety of organizations that collaborate with the sector to mitigate risk, including all levels of government, the private sector, international partners, and academia. Throughout the NIPP and the CIKR protection realm, these organizations are often referred to as "CIKR partners." This section provides a brief description of each of the key Chemical Sector partners and their roles and responsibilities in sector security.

1.2.1 U.S. Department of Homeland Security

Several offices and divisions within DHS have substantial responsibility for working with CIKR partners to mitigate security risks. In addition to being assigned the SSA for the sector, DHS also has several agencies and divisions with the authority to regulate security at chemical facilities, secure chemicals during transport, and ensure national cybersecurity, as well as provide important risk analysis and general program support. The following is a description of the roles and responsibilities for DHS Federal entities within the National Protection and Programs Directorate (NPPD), USCG, and TSA.

1.2.1.1 National Protection and Programs Directorate

The goal of NPPD is to advance the Department's risk-reduction mission. Reducing risk requires an integrated approach that encompasses both virtual and physical threats and their associated human elements. To address these threats, NPPD houses both the National Cyber Security Division (NCSD) and IP. IP comprises seven divisions, including the SSA Executive Management Office (EMO) and ISCD. The Chemical SSA is one of six SSAs assigned to the EMO. The Chemical SSA, ISCD, and NCSD are described in more detail below.

1.2.1.1.1 Chemical Sector-Specific Agency

The SSA is the primary Federal entity responsible for coordinating the unified public and private sector effort to protect against and mitigate the effects of natural or manmade events on the Chemical Sector. The SSA acts as a liaison among the private sector CIKR partners through the SCC and the public sector CIKR partners through the Government Coordinating Council (GCC) and the SLTTGCC. The SSA works with CIKR partners on a voluntary basis to develop, coordinate, and implement programs to increase chemical facility protection and resilience. The responsibilities of the Chemical SSA include the following:

- Implementing the NIPP;

- Encouraging risk management strategies that protect against and mitigate the effects of attacks against and other hazards to CIKR;

- Encouraging and supporting the development of information-sharing, analysis and sector-coordinating mechanisms;

- Encouraging and supporting the development of chemical security awareness and training initiatives;

- Facilitating information sharing regarding physical and cyber threats, vulnerabilities, incidents, potential protective measures, and commonly accepted practices; and

- Developing the CIKR Protection Sector Annual Report (SAR) and the Sector-Specific Plan.

1.2.1.1.2 Infrastructure Security Compliance Division

ISCD leads the implementation of CFATS, the Department's primary regulatory authority over security at the Nation's highest risk chemical facilities. In this role, ISCD faces the challenge of balancing the Nation's security needs against the importance of maintaining the economic vitality of the Chemical Sector. Chemical facilities regulated under CFATS may exist in any segment of the U.S. economy, including agriculture, healthcare and public health, universities and research institutions, and energy facilities. Some of the specific responsibilities of the ISCD under CFATS include the following:

- Developing and implementing a program that regulates the security of high-risk chemical facilities, including reviewing vulnerability assessments and site security plans developed by high-risk chemical facilities and performing compliance inspections to ensure that approved site security plans are being implemented;

- Promoting collaborative security planning through technical assistance and dialogue with covered facilities; and

- Implementing an information-protection program, with training and certification, to protect information developed under CFATS.

ISCD is also responsible for developing and overseeing compliance with regulations implementing the Secure Handling of Ammonium Nitrate Act. Under this authority, ISCD will, among other tasks, screen and issue registration numbers to individuals seeking to buy, sell, or transfer ammonium nitrate; develop and monitor compliance with point-of-sale requirements such as purchaser identification verification and recordkeeping; and issue guidance on identifying and responding to suspicious purchases of ammonium nitrate.

1.2.1.1.3 National Cyber Security Division

The DHS National Cyber Security Division (NCSD) serves as the national focal point for cybersecurity and collaborates with numerous components within DHS to provide the cross-sector information-sharing support and technical assistance necessary to best prepare for and respond to cyber events. As part of that effort, NCSD develops approaches and methodologies to assist organizations with protecting CIKR as identified in applicable laws and guidance. Within NCSD, several specialized programs focus on the Chemical Sector.

- The **Control Systems Security Program (CSSP)** is the lead program for industrial control system (ICS) cybersecurity activities in NCSD and DHS. CSSP has recently published the *Strategy for Securing Control Systems* as part of their overall mission to coordinate and lead efforts to improve control system security in the Nation's critical infrastructures. As part of this strategy, CSSP oversees several initiatives, including managing the Industrial Control Systems Joint Working Group (ICSJWG) to provide a formal mechanism to share information and foster the coordination of activities and programs across government and private sector stakeholders. CSSP also operates the Industrial Control Systems Cyber Emergency Response Team (ICS-CERT) to respond to incidents, analyze ICS-related vulnerabilities, and disseminate information and alerts to provide situational awareness and vulnerability mitigation strategies. In addition to these tasks, CSSP conducts instructor-led and Web-based security training courses and develops tools such as the Cyber Security Evaluation Tool (CSET).

- The **Critical Infrastructure Protection Cyber Security Program (CIP CS)** addresses the dual mission of coordinating IT Sector protection and promoting the security of cyber infrastructure across all sectors. CIP CS has created the Cross-Sector Cyber Security Working Group (CSCSWG) in order to facilitate cross-sector cybersecurity coordination. The Chemical Sector has been an active participant in this working group, as well as in the CSCSWG Metrics Subgroup, which identified potential cybersecurity goals, defined generic metrics, assessed the feasibility of each measure, and selected appropriate "sample" measures available for a majority of the sectors. The Metrics Subgroup also began to define the metadata to support the metrics. The Chemical Sector tailored these cyber metrics and will be reporting on them beginning in 2010.

1.2.1.2 The United States Coast Guard

Pursuant to MTSA, the USCG has authority over the security of chemical facilities that are adjacent to a navigable waterway, interface with regulated vessels, or could be involved in a transportation security incident. The law requires these facilities to conduct vulnerability assessments and develop security plans that may include security patrols, establishing restricted areas, personnel identification procedures, access control measures, and installation of surveillance equipment. Some responsibilities of the USCG relative to chemical facility security include the following:

- Implementing and enforcing the regulations according to MTSA;

- Conducting annual and spot compliance checks of all regulated maritime facilities, including chemical facilities with a maritime nexus;

- Reviewing and approving, or returning, FSPs; and

- Performing outreach to stakeholders to facilitate compliance and ensure consistent application of the regulations.

1.2.1.3 The Transportation Security Administration

TSA's Office of Transportation Sector Network Management (TSNM) leads the unified national effort to protect and secure our Nation's intermodal transportation systems. TSNM's mission is to reduce security risk in transportation and to promote the free flow of commerce by building a resilient, robust, and sustainable network with its public and private sector partners. The two organizational elements within TSNM that are most relevant to the transport of chemicals are the Highway and Motor Carrier Division and the Freight Rail Division.

The Freight Rail Division ensures the security of the Nation's freight rail network using a risk-informed approach. The division is responsible for leading teams of industry and government subject-matter experts to facilitate risk assessments related to the freight rail environment and help address mitigation strategies. The Highway and Motor Carrier Division leads the national effort to maintain the capability to move freely and facilitate commerce in the area of highway transportation security. Both divisions have developed voluntary security practices that address the transport of toxic inhalation hazard (TIH) and other security-sensitive materials. Many of the voluntary security practices have been incorporated into security regulations. Notable responsibilities of the TSA's Surface Transportation Team include the following:

- Leading efforts to reduce the vulnerability of security-sensitive materials in transportation;

- Developing and implementing rulemaking affecting rail and motor carriers;

- Providing guidance and training to shippers, receivers, and carriers of security-sensitive materials; and

- Conducting assessments of the chemical supply chain and providing assistance to foster security enhancements.

1.2.2 Other Federal Departments and Agencies

Pursuant to Homeland Security Presidential Directive 7 (HSPD-7), DHS has been charged with primary responsibility for coordinating CIKR protection in the Chemical Sector. There are numerous other Federal departments and agencies with responsibilities that are integral to overall sector risk management. DHS coordinates closely with these departments and agencies to perform necessary CIKR protection activities in the Chemical Sector more efficiently and effectively. As part of the NIPP, GCCs have been formed to serve as the formal entity for coordinating government-led sector CIKR protection activities. The GCC quarterly meetings provide an opportunity for public sector partners to update members on those CIKR protection activities that are important or relevant to the Chemical Sector. The roles and responsibilities of GCC member departments and agencies not previously mentioned can be found in Appendix 6A.

1.2.3 CIKR Owners and Operators

Given that virtually all infrastructure in the Chemical Sector is privately owned, owners and operators play a central role in sector CIKR protection. Ultimate implementation of security and preparedness measures reside within the private sector either through voluntary initiatives or driven by regulatory compliance. In addition to ownership and management of the vast majority of Chemical Sector infrastructure, the private sector is uniquely situated to provide the following important contributions to Chemical Sector protection and resilience:

- Implementation of a strong base of existing protection initiatives on which sector partners can build to enhance sector protection;

- Visibility into CIKR assets, systems, networks, facilities, and other capabilities;

- Ability to take actions to prepare for, respond to, and recover from incidents;

- Ability to innovate and to provide products, services, and technologies to focus on protection requirements; and

- Existing, robust mechanisms that are useful for sharing and protecting sensitive information regarding threats, vulnerabilities, countermeasures, and best practices.

Owners and operators also have various responsibilities to fulfill to ensure compliance with security regulations such as CFATS. Owners and operators are one of the driving forces behind a holistic approach to define security measures to include both physical security and cybersecurity in order to successfully implement CFATS at their facilities.

Interactions with owners and operators in the sector are achieved both directly and through their membership in the SCC member industry associations or State Chemical Industry Councils (CICs). The roles and responsibilities of these groups are described in more detail below.

1.2.3.1 Industry Associations and the Chemical Sector Coordinating Council

The Chemical Sector comprises numerous industry associations with which DHS works on a regular basis (see Appendix 6B). These associations have been extremely valuable partners, working informally with DHS since the Department was created in 2003 and in a formal capacity since the creation of the Chemical SCC in 2004. The SCC is the sector's mechanism for coordinating with DHS and is composed of representatives from 15 industry associations; however, the chair and vice chair are owners or operators. Based on the volume of products, the SCC represents a significant majority of the owners and operators in the Chemical Sector as defined by the SCC.

A number of Chemical SCC members participate on other SCCs, which provides a cross-sector perspective in sector activities and facilitates communication among interdependent sectors. Cross-sector activities include the following:

- The Chemical SCC developed and successfully implemented the Joint Hazardous Materials Rail Transportation Task Force with the Rail SCC (a Transportation Subsector);

- The Chemical SCC is working jointly with the Oil and Natural Gas (ONG) Subsector on an Emergency Response Subgroup; and

- The ONG SCC and the Highway and Motor Carrier SCC (a Transportation Subsector) both share members with the Chemical SCC.

The SCC also creates working groups to work collaboratively with the Chemical SSA on specific topics. The working groups may be active for a short time or for an extended period of time, depending on the issue. The following is a list of some of these working groups:

- The Chemical Sector-Specific Metrics Working Group developed a set of survey questions that will be used to report owner and operator metrics on an annual basis. This group will also determine the method in which the survey data will be collected and make any necessary future modifications.

- The SAR/Sector-Specific Plan Working Group collaborated with the SSA to draft the 2009 SAR, the 2009 Sector-Specific Plan Annual Update, and the 2010 Sector-Specific Plan.

- The Research and Development (R&D) Working Group has been established to provide a mechanism through which the private sector can interact with and obtain periodic updates on those Federal R&D projects that are of interest to the sector and identify capability gaps for the R&D process.

- The Chemical Sector Security Summit Working Group works with the Chemical SSA to develop an agenda and list of speakers for this annual conference.

1.2.3.2 State Chemical Industry Councils

While those industry associations who are members of the SCC represent a significant majority of the high-volume chemical manufacturers and distributors in the sector, they do not represent all companies in the sector. In order to reach a number of the small- to medium-sized companies, the Chemical SSA has engaged State CICs. The goals of State CICs typically encompass the following objectives:

- Providing timely and reliable information regarding the industry to the Governor, State legislatures, and various State agencies;

- Responding to the public and the media's need for reliable and useful information about the chemical industry;

- Speaking out on behalf of the industry regarding the importance of chemicals to the quality of life and the State's economy; and

- Promoting a coordinated chemical industry response on public policy issues and effective participation during the development of legislative and regulatory measures related to chemicals and science policy.

1.2.3.3 Chemical Information Technology Center Cyber Security Program

Established in 2005, the Chemical Information Technology Center (ChemITC) of the American Chemistry Council (ACC) provides a forum for ACC member companies to address common IT issues and support the industry's ability to safely and efficiently deliver products essential to society. The ACC ChemITC addresses maturing cybersecurity needs and serves as the industry's focal point for cybersecurity information, guidance, and tools. They offer assistance and coordinate with other chemical trade associations, such as the National Petrochemical and Refiners Association (NPRA) Cyber Security Subcommittee, as other associations organize their cybersecurity efforts.

In November 2008, a representative from the ACC ChemITC was invited to participate in SCC activities in a nonvoting capacity in order to keep the SCC informed of cybersecurity issues in the Chemical Sector. The ACC ChemITC focuses on the following strategic elements:

- Improving information sharing at the strategic, tactical, and operational levels throughout the industry, between the sector and DHS, and across CIKR sectors;

- Periodically reviewing cybersecurity guidance documents and making them available to assist chemical companies in enhancing their cybersecurity preparedness and performance, as well as compliance with the CFATS regulations;

- Working closely with other private sector partners on cybersecurity program and strategy development and implementation, including aiding in drafting documents, reviewing tools and associated materials, and serving as a subject-matter expert as needed;

- Working closely with IT and industrial automation and control system product and service providers to identify security and compliance needs and provide input on the challenges that chemical companies face in deploying products and solutions currently in use, as well as improving those in development; and

- Building on the industry's history of effective partnership with the government to articulate industry positions on chemical and cybersecurity legislation and provide a resource to government agencies on matters pertaining to cybersecurity in the Chemical Sector.

1.2.4 State, Local, Tribal, and Territorial Governments

State, local, tribal, and territorial authorities are integral to securing our Nation's infrastructure. They constitute the front line of defense in preventing harm and providing response when necessary to secure the Chemical Sector's critical infrastructure through public safety agencies such as local law enforcement, fire and rescue, emergency medical services, and emergency management. The Chemical Sector has a long history of coordinating with emergency responders and working with regulators at the State and local levels. DHS and the SSA have developed a strong, cooperative relationship with these groups primarily through the SLTTGCC and the State and major urban area fusion centers described below.

1.2.4.1 State, Local, Tribal, and Territorial Government Coordinating Council

Established in 2007, the SLTTGCC provides a forum for State, local, tribal, and territorial government homeland security directors or their equivalents to coordinate with the Federal Government and infrastructure owners and operators. Representatives from the SLTTGCC regularly attend the quarterly Chemical GCC meetings in order to receive the latest information on voluntary programs and activities in the sector, as well as updates to Federal regulations. State and local authorities are also invited to brief the GCC on State and local chemical-related CIKR protection issues as well.

In recognition of the importance of chemical security at the State and local levels, the SLTTGCC has created a CFATS Working Group to accomplish the following:

- Design an implementation process for the controlled dissemination of Chemical-terrorism Vulnerability Information (CVI) to appropriate State and local officials;

- Provide feedback on the CVI outreach program; and

- Develop and sustain an ongoing feedback process with CFATS implementation.

1.2.4.2 State and Major Urban Area Fusion Centers

Many States and larger cities have created State and major urban area fusion centers to share information and intelligence within their jurisdictions, as well as with the Federal Government. DHS provides personnel with operational and intelligence skills to the fusion centers who support the unique needs of the locality. These personnel strive to accomplish the following:

- Help the classified and unclassified information flow;

- Provide expertise;

- Coordinate with local law enforcement and other agencies;

- Establish relationships with CIKR owners and operators; and

- Provide local awareness and access.

The Chemical Sector is exploring how to best leverage these centers, especially during incidents. A list of fusion centers is included in Appendix 7.

1.2.5 Regional Consortium Coordinating Council

In an effort to coordinate CIKR protection efforts within geographic areas and across jurisdictional boundaries, the Regional Consortium Coordinating Council (RCCC) was formed in 2008. The mission of the RCCC is to strengthen regional collaboration to enhance protection, response, recovery, and resilience of the Nation's CIKR by accomplishing the following:

- Provide a means for DHS to interact with the various coalitions and partnerships across the country;

- Foster collaboration among the Nation's regional consortia so that best practices, lessons learned, and other means of support can be shared; and

- Address the Federal policy process so that protection and resilience efforts take geographic regions and sector interdependencies into account.

At this time, most of the RCCC collaborations are conducted through State and local councils. Although the Chemical Sector is not currently working with the RCCC on any joint protection efforts, because of their cross-sector and regional focus, the sector is open to participating in future projects with the RCCC.

1.2.6 International Organizations and Foreign Countries

The chemical industry is a global industry with many domestic facilities receiving raw materials, intermediate products, and equipment from foreign sources, as well as supplying these same resources to foreign customers. There is a particularly symbiotic relationship among chemical facilities located on both sides of the U.S.-Canadian and U.S.-Mexican borders. If one or more of these border facilities are shut down following an attack or other incident, adverse consequences would likely occur on the U.S. side of the border.

The main international concerns with regard to chemical protection include the potential impacts of a chemical spill or release in close proximity to any of the Nation's land borders; the cascading impacts of a disruption in the supply of materials, equipment, or services; and the threat to U.S.-owned assets abroad. The SSA has developed an international strategy with the mission to develop and foster partnerships with the international community in order to promote a global culture of protection and resilience in the Chemical Sector. This strategy includes the following:

- Fostering a dialogue with other countries (e.g., Australia, Canada, and the European Union) to promote a culture of international chemical security;

- Inviting members of the international chemical community to participate in the Chemical Sector Security Summit; and

- Compiling a list of chemical infrastructure vulnerability assessment methods and effective security planning strategies implemented by G-8 members.

Outreach efforts are also underway with DOS, which has recently joined the Chemical GCC. The GCC quarterly meetings provide an opportunity for DOS to discuss international chemical security programs with sector partners. These programs are being viewed in the broader context of reducing the global chemical threat.

The Chemical Sector is also engaging international partners in the area of cybersecurity. The ACC ChemITC is engaging with international organizations to share information on cybersecurity best practices, contribute to the development of international standards, and discuss possible future international collaboration.

1.2.7 Advisory Councils

Advisory councils provide advice, recommendations, and expertise to the government regarding CIKR protection policy and activities. They often provide an additional mechanism to share appropriate information with a preexisting group of private and public sector leaders thereby enhancing existing public-private partnerships. The following includes descriptions of notable organizations that provide advice to the sector.

1.2.7.1 Critical Infrastructure Partnership Advisory Council

The Critical Infrastructure Partnership Advisory Council (CIPAC) is a partnership between the Federal Government and private sector CIKR owners and operators that facilitates effective coordination of Federal CIKR protection programs pursuant to Section 121 of the Homeland Security Act and HSPD-7. The private sector members of CIPAC are members of the various CIKR SCCs, and the public sector members are DHS and members of the corresponding GCCs. While the purpose of CIPAC is more strategic and operational than advisory, DHS has exercised its authority under Section 871 of the Homeland Security Act to exempt CIPAC from the Federal Advisory Committee Act (FACA). This ensures that CIPAC members can discuss security-sensitive topics without the risk that these discussions could become public and jeopardize security. CIPAC can meet as a whole, or in the form of Joint Sector Committees specific to a particular sector.

1.2.7.2 National Infrastructure Advisory Council

Through the Secretary of Homeland Security, the National Infrastructure Advisory Council (NIAC) provides the President with advice on the security of physical and cyber systems across all CIKR sectors. NIAC is charged with improving cooperation and partnership between the public and private sectors in securing critical infrastructure. The council also holds the authority to provide advice directly to the heads of other agencies that have shared responsibility for CIKR protection.

NIAC provides advice on policies and strategies regarding risk assessment and management, information sharing, protective strategies, and clarification on roles and responsibilities between the public and private sector partners. The council typically studies four to six issues a year and strives to produce actionable recommendations in a timely manner. The White House monitors the progress of the council's studies on a regular basis through a liaison on the Homeland Security Council.

The council is composed of up to 30 members, appointed by the President, and meets four times a year in a public forum. Members are selected from the private sector, academia, and State and local governments.

1.2.7.3 Federal Senior Leadership Council

The Federal Senior Leadership Council (FSLC) is composed of senior leadership from each of the SSAs. Through regularly scheduled meetings, this organization addresses issues that are common among the 18 CIKR sectors, including cross-sector dependencies, policy issues, operational planning, and incident management.

1.2.7.4 CIKR Cross-Sector Council

The mission of the Partnership for Critical Infrastructure Security (PCIS) is to coordinate cross-sector initiatives that promote public and private efforts to help ensure secure, safe, and reliable critical infrastructure services across physical, cyber, and human elements. PCIS focuses primarily on cross-sector policy, strategy, and interdependency issues affecting the critical infrastructure sectors. These issues span the full spectrum of critical infrastructure concerns, from prevention, planning, and preparedness to business continuity, mitigation, response, and recovery. This collaborative forum enables asset owners and operators to work across sectors to address vital national safety and security issues in order to improve the security and resilience of the Nation's critical infrastructure.

PCIS, with support from the DHS Executive Secretariat, currently serves as the CIKR Cross-Sector Council within the sector partnership framework. The membership of the CIKR Cross-Sector Council includes the leadership from each of the SCCs, which represent the owners and operators of the CIKR within the sectors. Typically, the chair of each SCC serves as the member representative to the CIKR Cross-Sector Council.

1.2.8 Academia and Research Centers

The academic and research center communities play an important role in enabling national-level CIKR protection and implementation of the NIPP, including the following:

- Supporting the research, development, testing, evaluation, and deployment of CIKR protection technologies;

- Analyzing, developing, and sharing best practices related to CIKR protection efforts;

- Researching and providing innovative thinking and perspective on threats and the behavioral aspects of terrorism;

- Preparing or disseminating guidelines, courses, and descriptions of best practices for physical security and cybersecurity;

- Developing and providing suitable risk analysis and risk management courses for CIKR protection professionals; and

- Conducting research to identify new technologies and analytical methods that can be applied by sector partners to support the NIPP efforts.

The role of these organizations in the Chemical Sector focuses on chemical detection and analysis, chemical response and recovery, chemical characterization and toxicity, the safe transport of chemicals, and methods that protect the Nation's information infrastructure against catastrophic failures.

The Chemical SSA interacts with these and other organizations through the DHS S&T Integrated Product Teams (IPT). This process allows the sector to identify R&D capability gaps which are then incorporated into the larger S&T process. Gaps that can be transformed into projects are then included in the DHS S&T R&D portfolio to be considered for funding. A more in-depth discussion of these organizations and the R&D process is included in chapter 7.

1.3 Sector Mission, Vision, Goals, and Objectives

Figure 1-2: Establish Sector Goals and Objectives

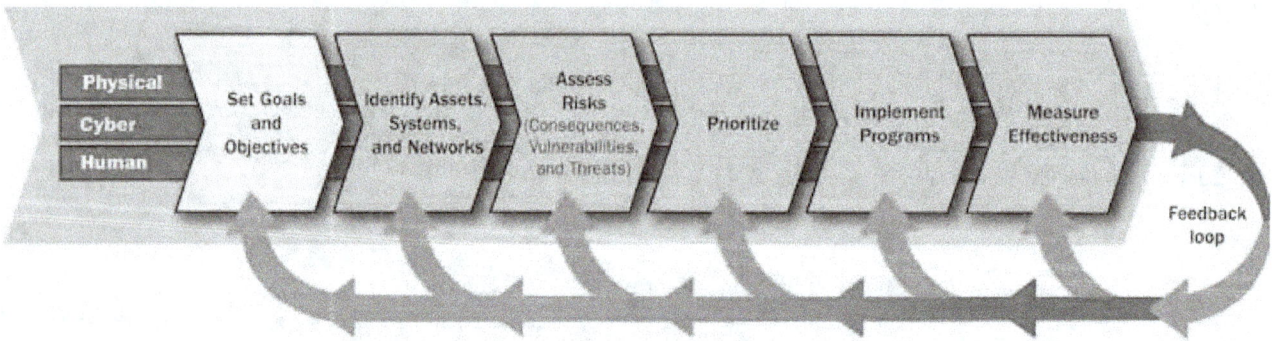

Continuous improvement to enhance protection of CIKR

Development of an overarching strategic planning framework begins with the development of the mission and vision statements. Once those statements are established, sector security goals and objectives can be crafted that focus on how the sector will achieve the ideal protective posture identified by the mission and vision statements (see Figure 1-2).

This document is informed by a variety of other documents, chief among them being the NIPP and the *National Strategy for Securing the Chemical Sector*. These documents have strategic planning elements that have an impact on the Chemical Sector's strategic planning. In the case of the NIPP, the goals and objectives are high-level goals and objectives that apply to all 18 CIKR sectors. Furthermore, the Chemical Sector-Specific Plan is an annex to the NIPP, and therefore is subordinate to the goals and objectives contained therein. In the *National Strategy for Securing the Chemical Sector*,[9] the Federal Government has set forth a strategic vision, strategic goals, strategic principles, and strategic actions for the sector. Collectively, these items greatly influence the strategic path of this Sector-Specific Plan and have been adopted as part of the Sector-Specific Plan's strategic planning framework.

The mission statement, vision statement, goals and objectives that have been developed for the Chemical Sector are discussed below. In the 2007 Sector-Specific Plan, these items were developed by DHS and supported by the SCC and the GCC. The mission and vision statements, goals, and objectives in this document were revised and developed in collaboration with sector partners. These groups will continue to work with DHS to implement activities in furtherance of the sector's strategic plan.

DHS, the SCC, and the GCC have agreed on the following mission statement for the Chemical Sector:

Mission Statement for the Chemical Sector

Reduce the Nation's chemical manufacturing and distribution infrastructure's vulnerability to all hazards based upon sound risk-based methodologies.

The DHS vision statement for the Chemical Sector, which was set forth in the *National Strategy for Securing the Chemical Sector*, has been revised and agreed to by the SCC and the GCC:

Vision Statement for the Chemical Sector

An economically competitive and increasingly resilient industry that achieves and maintains a sustainable security posture by effectively reducing vulnerabilities and consequences of all hazards, using risk-based assessments, industry best practices, and a comprehensive information-sharing environment between industry and government.

The Chemical Sector goals and objectives were first stated in the 2007 Chemical Sector-Specific Plan and were written using the NIPP risk management framework as a guide. The goals and objectives described the comprehensive, long-term protective posture that public and private sector partners were working together to achieve for the sector. Over the past three years, the partnership has matured along with the programs that have been implemented to strengthen the sector's desired protective posture. The Chemical SSA has worked closely with its CIKR partners to review and refine the sector goals and objectives to accurately reflect this new maturity. In addition, in accordance with new requirements outlined in the 2009 NIPP, the sector goals and objectives have been revised to consider all hazards and to ensure alignment with activities and progress as reported in the SAR. The revised Chemical Sector goals and objectives are listed in Table 1-2.

---

[9] As requested in the FY 2006 Homeland Security Appropriations Bill. The strategy was released in February 2006.

Table 1-2: Chemical Sector Goals and Objectives.

Goal 1. Evaluate the security posture of Chemical Sector high-risk assets, including physical, cyber, and human elements as needed.

- Update, as necessary, the sector definition and asset taxonomy to ensure that it aligns with industry's self-assessment of the sector.
- Maintain and update a catalogue of high-risk assets, including critical physical and cyber components within the Chemical Sector.
- Identify high-risk asset dependencies and interdependencies of critical domestic and international infrastructure that if disrupted would adversely critically impact the Nation's public health and safety, economic security, or national security.

Goal 2. Prioritize Chemical Sector critical infrastructure protection activities based on risk.

- Continue the implementation of the Chemical Facility Anti-Terrorism Standards and the Maritime Transportation Security Act, updating, as needed, the screening methodology and accompanying vulnerability assessments and site security plans that identify and protect those chemical assets, both physical and cyber, whose destruction or exploitation could potentially result in significant consequences.
- Evaluate consequence, vulnerability, and threat in a manner that supports sector and cross-sector comparison of risks by using a normalized risk-based assessment methodology.

Goal 3. Sustain risk-based, cost-effective sector-wide protective programs that increase asset-specific resilience without hindering the economic viability of the sector.

- Promote the sharing of best practices and lessons learned from voluntary and regulatory programs.
- Encourage emergency-related training drills to ensure preparedness and resilience against critical risks to CIKR protection.
- Increase the awareness of cybersecurity programs that encourage information sharing and implement programs that safeguard cyber systems.
- Develop and foster partnerships with the international community, as needed, to promote a global culture of security in the Chemical Sector.
- Develop and promote training and assessment tools for both physical security and cybersecurity.

Goal 4. Refine processes and mechanisms for ongoing government-private sector coordination to increase sector resilience, as necessary.

- Promote sector coordination and information sharing through the SCC and the GCC.
- Improve mechanisms to collect timely classified and unclassified information and to quickly disseminate the information in formats that can be shared with all sector security partners.
- Support the sector-wide use of an information-sharing network for the timely dissemination of Chemical Sector-specific information to security partners.
- Secure all proprietary, business, security-related, or other sensitive information shared with the Federal Government, including sector-wide use of information protection systems.

Goal 5. Support risk-based critical infrastructure protection R&D projects that add value to the Chemical Sector.

- Develop and establish a process to coordinate and share information on R&D projects with chemical CIKR partners.
- Identify risk-based R&D gaps, priorities, and affordable solutions.
- Prioritize projects based on industry need, threat, vulnerability, and consequence.

Goal 6. Measure the progress and effectiveness of sector critical infrastructure protection activities.

- Collect quantifiable information on the effectiveness of risk-reduction programs for inclusion in regular reports to DHS, Congress, the White House, the Chemical SCC, and other relevant security partners.

1.4 Value Proposition[10]

Efficiently and effectively securing the physical, cyber, and human elements of the Chemical Sector necessitates significant contributions of time, money, and other resources from all sector partners. For government partners, these expenditures are typically executively or legislatively mandated. However, under the NIPP partnership framework, private sector contributions are made voluntarily. Moreover, even high-risk chemical facilities that are required to meet various security standards can benefit from voluntarily participating in partnership activities designed to enhance overall sector protection and resilience. Partners participate in Chemical Sector protection efforts for the following reasons:

- Participation in a policy development and risk analysis and management framework helps focus both corporate and government planning and resource investment in asset protection;

- Influence regarding the type of environment (e.g., voluntary or regulatory) through which sector security is promoted;

- Improved partnerships with DHS and other government entities, regulating or otherwise engaged with the Chemical Sector, enabling the identification and communication of potential improvements in both voluntary and regulatory CIKR protection programs;

- Receipt of timely, accurate, and useful information on threats to Chemical Sector CIKR, protective best practices, assessment methodologies, and other information and tools that can help asset owners and operators better assess and protect their own assets and investments from all hazards;

- Greater information sharing regarding specific threats and hazards is enabled by the issuance of security clearances to private sector partners;

- Participation in national-level and cross-sector training and exercise programs will ensure that information sharing and restoration and recovery support of priority CIKR facilities are more effective during emerging threat and incident management situations;

- Enhanced cybersecurity postures can help prevent business and process interruption and the loss or misuse of proprietary information;

- Provision of a private sector perspective to R&D initiatives is needed to enhance future CIKR protection efforts; and

- Provision of platforms for private sector partners to:

  - Improve the internal and external understanding of efforts to reduce vulnerability through risk-based management practices and work processes; and

  - Demonstrate the social responsibility of the sector.

The value proposition is communicated and realized by taking advantage of the relationships outlined in Section 1.2. Chemical Sector partners meet regularly in a number of different forums to discuss a wide variety of issues important to the sector. The partnership model is a very collaborative process, which relies on input from all CIKR partners to improve the partnership, programs, and activities designed to mitigate risk in the sector. The suggestions are then incorporated, as warranted, to improve the effectiveness of the partnership and the programs.

---

[10] Value proposition refers to the direct benefits that both public and private sector partners realize through their participation in the public-private partnership.

2. Identify Assets, Systems, and Networks

DHS, in collaboration with CIKR partners, identifies the assets, systems, and networks that make up the Nation's CIKR in order to effectively manage critical infrastructure protection using a risk-based approach (see Figure 2-1).

Figure 2-1: Identify Assets, Systems, and Networks

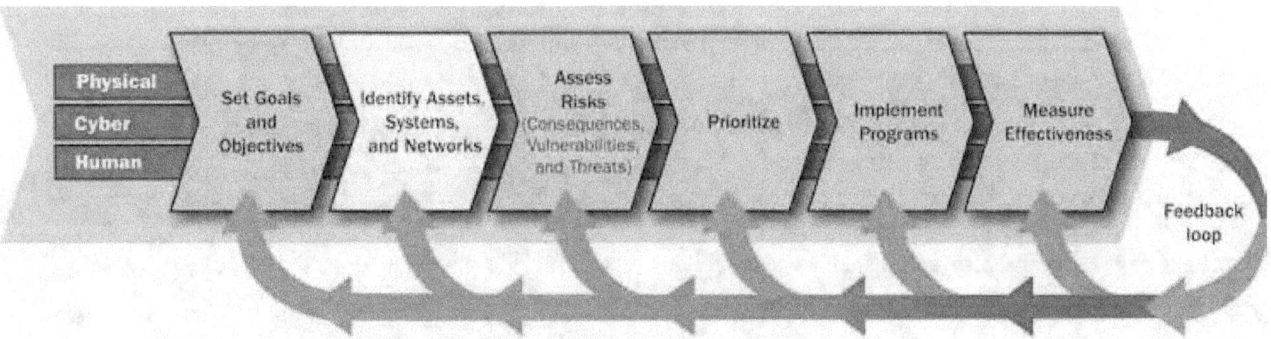

Continuous improvement to enhance protection of CIKR

The highest risk assets in the Chemical Sector are identified through the CFATS program and are based on specific chemicals of interest. In addition, other chemical facilities subject to USCG jurisdiction are covered under the MTSA regulatory programs. These programs have provided the main method through which the sector's CIKR information has been collected. Additional details on CFATS and MTSA are provided in chapter 1.

In order to manage the infrastructure information collected from all 18 sectors, DHS has created the Infrastructure Data Warehouse (IDW), a component of the Infrastructure Information Collection System (IICS). The IICS collects data from infrastructure information data sources and enables users to search, export, import, and manipulate data from a single access point. DHS also understands the need to protect and secure the information collected as a result of regulatory compliance, and has developed processes to collect and store infrastructure information that is respectful of regulations. This chapter discusses how DHS manages coordination of infrastructure information in order to identify assets in national programs utilizing the IDW.

The SSA also supports several voluntary programs that identify infrastructure in order to support risk management efforts in the sector. The Chemical and Hazardous Information Reference Portal (CHIRP) is a collaborative effort between the SSA and the States that uses information submitted as required by Title III of SARA. This information is being used to develop a database of sites around the country that store or use chemicals and has proven to be valuable during incidents to identify affected facilities and their emergency contact information.

A second voluntary program is a collaborative effort between DHS and the private sector that identifies critical control and business systems in the Chemical Sector. As a result of this voluntary collaboration, a roadmap was produced that outlines a comprehensive plan to improve the security, reliability, and functionality of industrial control systems over the next several years. No infrastructure information is collected in a centralized location, instead, the roadmap design assists owners and operators in identifying the systems that are important to their business and provides a plan for them to improve the security of their cyber assets.

While it is important to identify critical assets, systems, and networks, ensuring that processes are in place to verify and update this information is essential. This chapter concludes with a discussion of these processes, as well as the programs developed to protect and secure this information.

2.1 The Infrastructure Data Warehouse

In accordance with the 9/11 Commission Act, DHS is the lead coordinator in the national effort to identify the country's CIKR. To facilitate the compilation and management of the Nation's infrastructure data, DHS created the IDW, a component of the IICS, which is maintained by IP's Infrastructure Information Collection Division (IICD). The IDW is the Federal Government's repository for information on the evolving, comprehensive inventory of assets, systems, and networks that make up the Nation's critical infrastructure and key resources. These assets, systems, and networks may be significant at a national level or important to State, local, or regional CIKR protection, incident management, and response and recovery efforts. The IDW is not a prioritized list of the Nation's critical infrastructure; however, the data is searchable in a variety of ways and can be used to create prioritized lists based on selected parameters.

The IICS will use data managed by the IDW to provide users with access to the most up-to-date, comprehensive source of critical infrastructure data. Users will be able to search, store, and retrieve infrastructure data from multiple sources and, ultimately, be able to collaborate and share knowledge about data attributes in order to enhance and improve data quality.

Although data-collection processes are still under development in the sector, the goal of the IDW is to provide access to relevant information for events such as natural disasters, industrial accidents, and other incidents. The IDW will also maintain basic information about the relationships, dependencies, and interdependencies among various assets, systems, and networks, including foreign CIKR, on which the United States may rely. Risk may change based on many factors, including damage resulting from a natural disaster; seasonal or cyclical dependencies; and changes in technology, the economy, or the terrorist threat. The inventory supports domestic incident management by helping perform the following tasks:

- Focusing preparedness planning;

- Informing decision making;

- Establishing strategies for response; and

- Informing the restoration, remediation, and reconstruction processes.

Table 2-1: Infrastructure Data Warehouse Data Elements

General Data Fields
Name of Asset • Primary Street Address • City • State • ZIP Code
Geographic Location • Latitude and Longitude
Infrastructure Data Taxonomy Information • Sector • Subsector (if applicable)
Asset Owner
Asset Operator
Asset Point of Contact • Name • Address • Telephone Number • E-mail Address

At this time, the IDW, as described above, applies to those sector assets determined to be critical but not subject to security regulations. The comprehensive information on Chemical Sector CIKR that is collected through security regulations is not currently contained in the IDW. Information on this infrastructure is under the protection and control of the implementing divisions. As a result of these restrictions, IICD is collaborating with these divisions to develop a process to collect asset information while also respecting the regulatory data-protection programs.

2.1.1 Defining Information Parameters

As a first step in identifying sector infrastructure, DHS defined the specific types of information that it seeks to collect about each type of infrastructure regardless of sector, subsector, or segment. These general data fields are broad enough to support the entire range of CIKR protection activities for which the IDW serves as an information source. The general data fields requested for all infrastructure, regardless of type, are listed in Table 2-1.

2.1.2 Infrastructure Data Taxonomy for the Chemical Sector

The Infrastructure Data Taxonomy (IDT) provides a common framework that promotes an efficient integration and transfer of information, as well as an effective analytic framework for comparison. Over the past several years, the IDT has been improved and refined to better align with industry's self-assessment and experience. The IDT is used by DHS to identify, collect, and catalogue infrastructure data for the Chemical Sector, as well as all other CIKR sectors. Table 2-2 contains a list of the Chemical Sector IDT that was approved by sector partners in 2008.

Table 2-2: Infrastructure Data Taxonomy for the Chemical Sector

3. Chemical and Hazardous Materials Industry	
3.1	Chemical Manufacturing and Processing Plants
3.1.1	Basic Chemicals
3.1.1.1	Inorganic Chemicals
3.1.1.1.1	Alkalies and Chlorine
3.1.1.1.2	Industrial Gases
3.1.1.1.3	Inorganic Pigments
3.1.1.1.4	Acids
3.1.1.1.5	Other Inorganics
3.1.1.2	Petrochemicals and Derivatives
3.1.1.2.1	Organics
3.1.1.2.2	Synthetic Materials
3.1.1.2.3	Other Organics
3.1.1.3	Other Industrial Chemicals

3. Chemical and Hazardous Materials Industry	
3.1.2	Specialty Chemicals
3.1.2.1	Coatings
3.1.2.2	Other Specialties
3.1.2.3	Explosives
3.1.3	Agricultural Chemicals
3.1.3.1	Fertilizers
3.1.3.2	Crop Protection
3.1.3.2.1	Pesticides
3.1.3.2.2	Herbicides
3.1.3.2.3	Other Crop Protection Chemicals
3.1.4	Pharmaceuticals
3.1.5	Consumer Products
3.1.6	Potential Chemical Weapon Agents and Precursors
3.2	Hazardous Chemical Transport
3.2.1	Pipelines
3.2.1.1	Pipeline Components
3.2.1.2	Pipeline Pumping Stations
3.2.1.3	Pipeline Control Centers
3.2.2	Marine Transport
3.2.2.1	Tankers[a]
3.2.2.2	Ports Handling Chemicals
3.2.3	Rail Transport
3.2.3.1	Railroad Tank Cars[a]
3.2.3.2	Railroad Loading Racks
3.2.4	Road Transport[b]

3. Chemical and Hazardous Materials Industry	
3.2.4.1	Tanker Trucks
3.2.4.2	Tanker Truck Loading Racks
3.2.5	Air Transport
3.3	Hazardous Chemical Storage/Stockpile/Utilization/Distribution
3.3.1	Warehousing and Storage
3.3.1.1	Bulk Storage
3.3.1.1.1	Land-Based Terminal
3.3.1.1.2	Marine Terminal
3.3.1.2	Retail Distribution
3.3.2	Storage at Manufacturing Facilities
3.3.3	Storage at Non-Manufacturing Facilities
3.4	Regulatory, Oversight, and Industry Organizations
3.4.1	Federal Chemicals Oversight Agencies
3.4.2	Regional, State, Local, Tribal, and Territorial Agencies
3.4.3	Chemical Industry Organizations and Trade Associations
3.4.4	International Chemical Organizations
3.5	Other Hazardous Chemical Facilities

[a] Includes intermodel containers.

[b] Also includes cargo trucks, intermodel containers, and truck trailers.

2.2 Collecting Infrastructure Information

2.2.1 Chemical Facility Anti-Terrorism Standards (CFATS)

The primary method for collecting data on CIKR deemed to be high risk in the Chemical Sector is through the CFATS regulatory program. This program is the primary means through which critical physical and cyber assets, systems, and networks are identified. In order to collect and analyze the information submitted by facilities subject to the regulation, DHS developed CSAT, a suite of online programs to accept and analyze information submitted in response to CFATS. DHS utilizes the CSAT suite of tools to perform the following tasks:

1. Gather information on facilities that are likely to present a high level of security risk based on the quantities of chemicals of interest possessed onsite by the facility;

2. Support the Department's preliminary and final tiering decisions for potential high-risk chemical facilities;

3. Facilitate the submission and assessment of a chemical facility's security vulnerabilities via the SVA; and

4. Support the intake and evaluation of high-risk chemical facility Site Security Plans.

In February 2008, DHS began analyzing the submitted Top-Screens to identify the preliminary tier and the risk associated with individual facilities, and to identify the facilities that are required to submit SVAs or, for Tier 4 facilities, ASPs. To date, DHS has received and reviewed more than 38,000 Top-Screens and has identified approximately 7,000 facilities as preliminary high-risk chemical facilities. The due date for an SVA or ASP is based on the date upon which the facility received its preliminary risk tier, with the initial group of SVAs due in January 2009. To date, DHS has received more than 6,000 SVAs.

2.2.2 Maritime Transportation Security Act (MTSA)

Some Chemical Sector CIKR assets are regulated under MTSA, which has jurisdiction over the security of chemical facilities located on, or adjacent to, U.S. waters. This authority requires the USCG to collect and maintain essential infrastructure information concerning these facilities and review and approve FSAs and FSPs.

2.2.3 National Critical Infrastructure Prioritization Program (NCIPP)

Through authorities in the 9/11 Commission Act of 2007, DHS is the lead coordinator in the national effort to identify the country's CIKR. DHS executes this responsibility through the National Critical Infrastructure Prioritization Program (NCIPP), which is administered by the Homeland Infrastructure Threat and Risk Analysis Center (HITRAC). The program is intended to identify the Nation's most critical, highly consequential domestic assets and systems from all 18 sectors in order to support the growing DHS role during incident response and recovery. HITRAC coordinates with the individual governmental entities to gain access to critical infrastructure information collected in response to the regulations mentioned above while also complying with the applicable data-protection programs.

Due to valuable input from both private and public sector partners at the State and local levels, this program has evolved into a list of lists, including the following for the Chemical Sector:

• The NCIPP Level 1 and Level 2 comprise those critical assets that are regulated by CFATS or MTSA and also meet the NCIPP Level 1 and Level 2 criteria as listed in Table 2-3.

• The sector list includes CIKR that meet one or more of the following criteria:

  – NCIPP Level 1 and Level 2 CIKR;

  – Chemical facilities that are the sole source of production of an important chemical; or

  – CIKR clusters that are geographically important or are interdependent due to the use of an important chemical.

- State and territory lists include CIKR that are important at the State and territorial levels. In addition to individual CIKR, clusters of CIKR may also be included as discussed above.

Every year, DHS requests that State and territorial partners propose CIKR for inclusion on the NCIPP lists. All proposals are provided to the SSA for consideration for the NCIPP Level 1 and Level 2 lists. Infrastructure proposed by States and Territories for the NCIPP Level 1 and Level 2 lists and State and Territory lists are provided to the respective Homeland Security Advisors. Following the initial data call, the reconsideration and adjudication process begins. During this phase, DHS facilitates dialogue among State, Territory, and sector partners, as necessary, to discuss the nominations and to solicit additional information in support of reconsideration requests.

The Chemical SSA also provided an opportunity for sector CIKR partners to participate in the NCIPP CFDI. This initiative was developed in close collaboration with DOS, as well as with other partners in the critical infrastructure protection and intelligence communities to identify assets and systems outside the United States that are critical to the Nation's public health, economic, or national security. The SSA will continue to engage public and private sector partners in order to identify CIKR that meet the CFDI criteria.

Table 2-3: Criteria for NCIPP Level 1 and Level 2 Infrastructure

NCIPP Level 1	NCIPP Level 2
Those CIKR that, if disrupted, could result in at least two of the following consequences:	Those CIKR that, if disrupted, could result in at least two of the following consequences:
1. Greater than 5,000 prompt fatalities. 2. Greater than $75 billion in first-year economic consequences. 3. Mass evacuations with a prolonged absence of greater than 3 months. 4. Severe degradation of the country's national security capabilities, including intelligence and defense functions, but excluding military facilities.	1. Greater than 2,500 prompt fatalities. 2. Greater than $25 billion in first-year economic consequences. 3. Mass evacuations with a prolonged absence of greater than 1 month. 4. Severe degradation of the country's national security capabilities, including intelligence and defense functions, but excluding military facilities.

2.2.4 Chemical HAZMAT Information Reference Portal

The SSA developed a voluntary collection effort to support incident management activities during natural or manmade disasters, as well as National Level Exercises. CHIRP is a collaborative effort between the Chemical SSA and the States to provide a secure data portal for chemical information on sites that must comply with EPA RMP reporting requirements and Title III of SARA. The SSA collaborated with the EPA to provide the publicly available RMP data for all 50 States and U.S. Territories. The SSA is currently collaborating with individual States to collect SARA Title III information to be included in the portal.

CHIRP links critical site information with chemical inventories, chemical hazards information based on the inventory, and emergency contact information for each site. The secure portal has been a valuable tool during incidents to assist with identifying infrastructure in an affected area that may not be considered a high security risk, but nonetheless, is locally significant.

2.2.5 Roadmap to Secure Control Systems in the Chemical Sector

The sector is currently engaged in a voluntary, public-private sector collaboration to identify and reduce the risk to critical cyber assets at CIKR facilities. This effort has produced a roadmap addressing cybersecurity issues, challenges, and goals for improvement in areas specifically related to industrial control systems owned and operated by commercial chemical industries. Industrial control systems are critical cyber assets that have become an essential element in the management of complex chemical processes and production environments.

Building on existing government and industry efforts to improve the security of industrial control systems within the private sector, the roadmap achieves the following:

- Defines a consensus-based strategy that addresses the specific cybersecurity needs of owners and operators of CIKR facilities;

- Proposes a comprehensive plan, which includes goals and milestones, for improving the security, reliability, and functionality of industrial control systems over the next 10 years;

- Guides the efforts of industry, academia, and government; and

- Promotes continuous improvement in the security posture of critical industrial control systems.

Although working toward implementation of this roadmap is voluntary, it does align with the CFATS methodology of RBPS for securing critical cyber assets.

Over the next several years, the Chemical Sector will pursue a coordinated approach that aligns current activities to roadmap goals and milestones; initiates specific projects to address critical gaps; and provides a mechanism for collaboration, project management, oversight, and information sharing among the sector stakeholders. The approach aims to clearly define activities, projects, and initiatives that contain time-based deliverables tied to roadmap goals and milestones.

2.3 Verifying Infrastructure Information

Given the number of chemical facilities in the United States, DHS does not have the resources to verify infrastructure information on all chemical facilities. However, the highest risk assets in the Chemical Sector will be verified through one of the regulatory programs described below.

2.3.1 CFATS

DHS has the authority to verify information submitted as part of the CFATS regulatory program through on-site inspections. To conduct inspections, DHS has developed a trained cadre of Chemical Security Inspectors. Chemical Security Inspectors will periodically visit regulated facilities to verify the information submitted by each facility in its SVA and Site Security Plan. The timing and structure of inspections will vary based on the tier level of the covered facility. Facilities will be inspected at regular intervals, with higher risk tiered facilities being inspected first and more frequently. DHS may also inspect a facility at any time based on new information or specific security concerns.

2.3.2 MTSA

The USCG was granted the authority to verify information submitted as part of the MTSA regulatory program through documented audits and compliance visits. USCG facility inspectors visit regulated facilities for the purpose of verifying information submitted as part of their approved FSP. The regulations require a minimum of two compliance visits to each facility per year; one visit is unannounced. The regulations also require a yearly documented audit of the FSP.

To assist in ensuring that information submitted under MTSA is accurate, Congress granted the USCG the authority to assess a civil penalty per violation of MTSA.

2.4 Updating Infrastructure Information

Depending on the regulatory program, there are several ways for CIKR partners to update their infrastructure information with DHS should a significant change occur at their facility. For programs such as CHIRP, the SSA is able to take advantage of regulations administered by other Federal agencies to ensure that infrastructure information is updated.

2.4.1 CFATS

For those facilities covered by CFATS, the rule specifies a schedule for initial submission of the CSAT Top-Screen, SVA, and Site Security Plan, as well as for periodic resubmission of these documents. How frequently these documents must be updated and resubmitted depends on the document in question and the risk level of the facility. Section 27.210 of the interim final rule states that DHS will require facilities in Tiers 1 and 2 to update their Top-Screen, SVA, and Site Security Plan every two years, and facilities in Tiers 3 and 4 to update their Top-Screen, SVA, and Site Security Plan every three years.

In addition to the periodic updates required under CFATS, the regulation provides that if a covered facility makes a "material modification" to its operations, the covered facility must complete and submit a revised Top-Screen to DHS within 60 days of completion of the material modification. Material modifications can include a variety of changes, and thus DHS cannot provide an exhaustive list of items that would be considered material modifications. In general, DHS expects that material modifications would likely include the following:

- Changes at a facility to chemical holdings, including the presence of a new chemical, an increased amount of an existing chemical, or the modified use of a given chemical; or

- Changes to the site's physical configuration, which may

  - Substantially increase the level of consequence should a terrorist attack or incident occur;

  - Substantially increase a facility's vulnerabilities from those identified in the facility's SVA;

  - Substantially affect the information already provided in the facility's Top-Screen submission; or

  - Substantially affect the measures contained in the facility's Site Security Plan.

In accordance with the resubmission requirements in section 27.210(b)(2) and (3), and following review of the facility's resubmitted Top-Screen, the Department will notify the covered facility as to whether the covered facility must also submit a revised SVA, Site Security Plan, or both.

2.4.2 MTSA

According to the regulations outlined in MTSA, the FSP submitted by a regulated facility is valid for five years from the date of approval by the local Captain of the Port (COTP). At the end of five years, a regulated facility must submit a renewal of their FSP to be reviewed and approved by the local COTP. A regulated facility that wishes to make substantive changes to their approved FSP is required to provide the proposed changes to the COTP for approval before those changes can be implemented.

2.4.3 NCIPP

On an annual basis, the SSA works with its CIKR partners to collect current information on those assets that appear on or have been proposed for the Level 1, Level 2, and Sector Lists. CIKR that have been proposed for the Individual State and Territory Lists are provided through the Homeland Security Advisors (HSAs). HSAs work directly with representatives from the States and the Territories to ensure that the data submitted are accurate.

The majority of the infrastructure on the Chemical Sector NCIPP lists is regulated by CFATS or MTSA. The facilities identified in the NCIPP that are also covered by these regulations have a regulatory requirement to update their information with DHS as described in Sections 2.4.1 and 2.4.2.

2.4.4 CHIRP

The SSA is currently engaging individual States to incorporate their infrastructure information into the CHIRP database. The infrastructure information that the SSA is compiling is being collected in order to satisfy the reporting requirements of existing regulations. Facility information contained in the CHIRP is updated based on one of the following two conditions:

1. Facility information submitted under SARA Title III reporting requirements must be submitted annually to the State in which the facility or site resides.

2. Facility information submitted under the EPA RMP must be reviewed every 5 years or updated as required in 40 CFR 68.190. For example, if a facility's emergency contact information should change, the regulations require the facility to update their RMP within a month of the change.

2.5 Protection of Infrastructure Information

Much of the information collected as part of the NIPP risk management effort is sensitive from either a business or security perspective. Accordingly, the security of the submitted information is extremely important. DHS and other Federal agencies have developed a number of programs and procedures to ensure that CIKR information is properly safeguarded. Some of these programs have been developed in coordination with security regulations in order to protect the information that is submitted in compliance with the regulations. The information protection programs important to protecting chemical security information are briefly described in this section. These and other information protection programs will be discussed in more detail in Section 8.4.

CVI protects information that facilities develop for the purposes of complying with CFATS. CVI may be shared with State and local government officials or other individuals if the official or other individual (1) is CVI certified and (2) has a need to know the CVI.

SSI is used by the USCG, TSA, and DOT to protect the following types of information:

• Information that is detrimental to security;

• Information that reveals trade secrets or privileged or confidential information; or

• Information that constitutes an unwarranted invasion of privacy.

The SSI program is managed by DHS TSA and the SSI protection applies to both government officials and Transportations Systems Sector owners and operators with a demonstrated need to know.

The Protected Critical Infrastructure Information (PCII) Program protects information voluntarily shared with the Federal Government. When validated and marked as PCII, the information is exempt from public disclosure and must be properly accessed, used, and safeguarded. The program includes specific requirements for submitting critical infrastructure information, as well as requirements that governmental entities must meet for accessing and safeguarding PCII.

3. Assess Risks

Managing and mitigating risk is a cornerstone of CIKR protection and resilience efforts under the NIPP. To organize and prioritize these efforts, DHS adopted the risk management methodology that risk to an asset, system, or network is a function of the likely consequences of a successful attack (C), the vulnerability to attack (V), and the likelihood or threat of an attack (T). The risk methodology is expressed as:

Risk (R) = f { Consequence (C), Vulnerability (V), Threat (T) }

This chapter will discuss the Chemical Sector's past, present, and future approaches to assessing sector infrastructure using a risk-based approach (see Figure 3-1).

Figure 3-1: Assess Risks (Consequences, Vulnerabilities, and Threats)

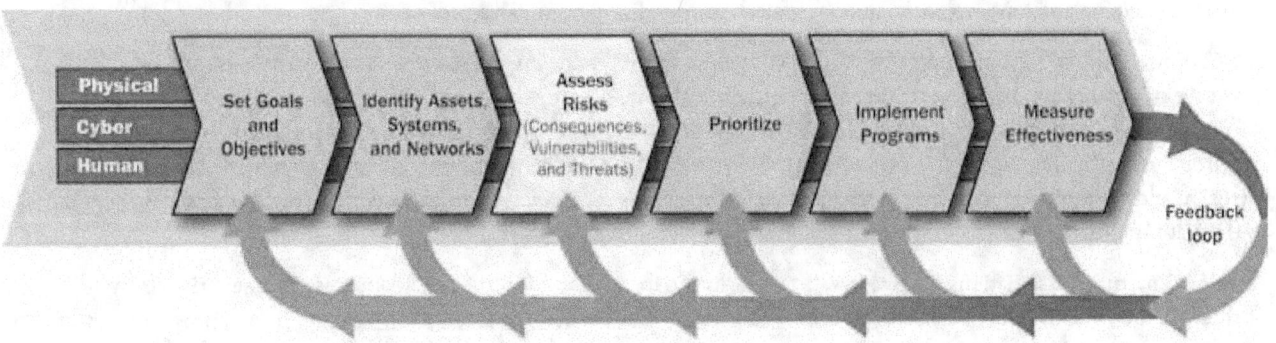

Continuous improvement to enhance protection of CIKR

3.1 Use of Risk Assessment in the Sector

The Chemical Sector has a long history and extensive experience developing and applying various methodologies and tools to assess facility risk and prioritize assets. Such methodologies have been developed by a variety of sector partners, including professional and industry trade associations, national research laboratories, and individual chemical companies. For several decades, facility owners and operators have been required by regulation to perform risk assessments of their facilities as they pertain to safety, process safety, and environmental issues. Assessments are required to ensure that baseline safety and environmental measures are employed at locations where HAZMAT in certain threshold amounts are used or maintained. Under the direction of other Federal agencies and regulatory requirements, the private sector used different processes and terminologies to determine risk than those applied more recently by DHS. For example, following the lead of other industries such as insurance and finance, risk was defined as Probability (P) x Consequence (C). Threat and vulnerability were understood to be included as a part of "Probability."

In response to the September 11th attacks, Congress passed MTSA in 2002 to address the vulnerability of the Nation's ports and waterways as they pertain to transportation security. Under MTSA, facilities adjacent to navigable waterways are required to perform a vulnerability assessment and develop an FSP, which must be approved by the local COTP. Likewise, the regulation creates Area Maritime Security Committees under the COTP's chairmanship that are made up of port stakeholders, as well as Federal, State, and local representatives. The role of the committee is to develop overarching assessments and security plans for the broader port complex in each COTP zone. The COTP and port stakeholders use the Maritime Security Risk Assessment Model (MSRAM) to perform detailed scenario risk assessments on all CIKR at the local port level. The model also provides the capability to compare different targets and geographic areas at the national, regional, and local levels.

Additionally, as part of the CFATS effort discussed in chapters 1 and 2, high-risk facilities must provide DHS with sufficient consequence and vulnerability information to make determinations as to each facility's security risk level.

The sector also actively promotes numerous voluntary efforts to assess the vulnerability and risk of physical and cyber infrastructure. These efforts include those led by industry associations, many of which support and promote security vulnerability assessments as part of their security guidance for member companies. The security guidance also provides association members with information on industry best practices to improve overall physical security and cybersecurity.

Efforts to assess risk in the sector also include cooperative partnerships among asset owners and operators, industry associations, and the Federal Government. One such effort is the Strategic Homeland Infrastructure Risk Assessment (SHIRA).[11] SHIRA provides senior decisionmakers with sector-specific and cross-sector assessments of various risks to the Nation's CIKR sectors. The assessment is a model that evaluates the threat from specific attack methods, the vulnerability of the CIKR to the attack methods, and the consequences of a most likely, worst case attack. Physical and cyber attacks made by terrorists, nation-states, malicious insiders, and lone-wolf assailants, as well as natural disasters, are assessed.

The Chemical SSA, owners and operators, and members of the SCC and GCC are asked to identify those physical and cyber threat scenarios that are of greatest concern to the Chemical Sector. Sector partners provide vulnerability and consequence information for these scenarios that is specific to the Chemical Sector. This information is then combined with threat information from across the Intelligence Community to create a Sector Risk Profile in order to identify the highest risk scenarios for the sector. In addition to a sector-specific assessment, SHIRA provides senior decisionmakers with a cross-sector assessment of risks to the Nation's CIKR.

Some SCC member associations have reservations about the method used in the SHIRA process to assess risk. In spite of these challenges, the Chemical SSA is working to increase the participation of sector partners in this program. Sector partners provide valuable information to assess sector vulnerabilities and consequences, and provide valuable suggestions to improve the SHIRA process.

Due to the sensitivity of the analysis, the SHIRA report is classified at the Secret level, but is made available to CIKR sector owners and operators and other sector partners with the appropriate clearance and need to know. DHS encourages infrastructure protection community partners to use the HITRAC threat information and risk assessments to inform their infrastructure protection activities.

---

[11] SHIRA was the methodology developed in response to a Presidential directive to compare and prioritize risks to assets within and across infrastructure sectors. In addition, the sector risk profiles generated from the SHIRA process satisfy reporting requirements for the National CIKR Annual Report.

Sector partners also worked collaboratively to develop the Voluntary Chemical Assessment Tool (VCAT). VCAT is a secure, Web-based application designed for use by nonregulated chemical facilities. The tool allows owners and operators to identify their facility's current risk level using an all-hazards approach and facilitates cost-benefit analysis by allowing them to select the best combination of physical security countermeasures and mitigation strategies to reduce overall risk. While regulated facilities have also found this tool to be helpful, it is not affiliated with CFATS or MTSA.

The risk assessment tools used in the Chemical Sector follow many of the same widely accepted steps. The steps include the following:

1. Initial screening of infrastructure to determine those assets that warrant a detailed risk assessment;

2. Determining the potential consequences of a successful attack (C);

3. Identifying the vulnerabilities related to the specific infrastructure (V); and

4. Determining the threat to or attractiveness of the specific infrastructure (T).

Each of these steps is discussed in greater detail below.

3.2 Screening Infrastructure

Chemical facility owners and operators know which assets at individual sites are the most important or critical to their operations. Many of them use one of the increasingly available tools to assess the vulnerability of the most critical assets. However, in light of the large number of chemical facilities spread throughout the Nation, it is not practical to require that comprehensive risk assessments be conducted at every chemical facility. Therefore, a screening should occur to identify which facilities warrant the expenditure of resources necessary for detailed risk assessments as outlined in Federal regulations.

This section contains a discussion of the screening methodologies as authorized by the CFATS and MTSA regulations, as well as several approaches used by the private sector.

3.2.1 CFATS

The CFATS Appendix A: DHS Chemical of Interest List was published in the Federal Register on November 20, 2007, and contains a list of chemicals of interest and their Screening Threshold Quantity (STQ). Possession of one or more of these chemicals of interest at or above the applicable threshold quantity triggers a requirement for the facility to complete and submit a Top-Screen. The Top-Screen is part of the suite of on-line programs in CSAT, discussed previously in Section 2.2.1. The data gathered through the Top-Screen tool informs DHS's initial determination of the facility's level of risk and the potential need for the facility to comply with the substantive requirements of CFATS.

Approximately 38,000[12] facilities have completed the Top-Screen. Of those, about 7,000 facilities were preliminarily determined by DHS to be high risk. Those facilities received preliminary tiering decisions and were instructed to complete CSAT SVAs or, where appropriate, an ASP in lieu of an SVA. Based on an analysis of the SVA or ASP, DHS will make a decision on the facility's final status as high risk. If DHS determines that a facility is, in fact, high risk, DHS will then provide the facility with its final risk-based tier. Alternatively, DHS will inform the facility that it is not high risk and is thus excluded from CFATS coverage at that time. Any facility assigned to a final tier must complete a CSAT Site Security Plan, or ASP, subject to DHS review and approval, demonstrating how the facility will meet the CFATS RBPS.

The screening of potentially high-risk chemical facilities is an ongoing process due to changes in factors such as the economic environment, business priorities, product inventories, and manufacturing processes. Any facility that comes into possession

---

[12] As of April 30, 2010.

of a chemical listed in CFATS Appendix A at or above the applicable STQ must complete and submit a CSAT Top Screen. DHS continues to review submitted Top-Screens and SVAs.

3.2.2 MTSA

Under MTSA, those facilities that meet the applicability provisions in 33 CFR 105.105 are essentially "screened" into the regulatory process and must comply with the regulations. Generally, these include chemical facilities that

- Handle explosives, liquefied natural or hazardous gas, or other Certain Dangerous Cargoes (CDCs);
- Transfer oil or hazardous materials;
- Handle cargo vessels greater than 100 gross register tons; and
- Handle barges that carry cargoes regulated by 46 CFR, Chapter 1, subchapter D or O or CDCs.

Facilities that meet the applicability provisions must conduct an FSA and submit an FSP to the USCG for approval.

3.2.3 Private Sector Efforts

Many of the industry associations who are members of the SCC strongly encourage their member companies to perform risk assessments or require risk assessments as an element of membership. Some industry associations mandating risk assessments also provide a screening methodology to determine what level of assessment should be performed at specific facilities. Risk may be assessed by focusing primarily on the intrinsic properties of the chemicals, such as toxicity, flammability, or other specific properties that may make a chemical an attractive target. Others assess risk by first calculating a Security Risk Index (SRI) based on risk factors such as the difficulty of the attack (D), the severity of the attack (S), and the attractiveness of the target (A). Ultimately, the facilities are assigned to categories from the highest risk to the lowest risk based on guidance provided by the industry association (see example, Table 3-1).

Table 3-1: Sample Security Risk Index (SRI) Calculation

Difficulty (D) + Severity (S) + Attractiveness (A) = Security Risk Index (SRI)			
Relative Difficulty of Attack (D)[a]	Relative Severity of Attack (S)[b]	Attractiveness of Target (A)[c]	Security Risk Index (SRI)
1	1	1	
2	(2)	2	
(3)	3	3	3 + 2 + 4 = (9)
4	4	(4)	

[a] Difficulty of attack refers to the type of attack scenario, with 1 representing a well-planned, coordinated series of events requiring access to restricted areas and 4 representing an attack scenario that could be accomplished by a single individual with readily available equipment or materials.

[b] Severity of attack is in terms of population density within the radius of attack, with 1 being a low population density and 4 being the highest population density.

[c] Refers to factors that influence the attractiveness of the target, with 1 representing an attack with limited localized concern and 4 impacting the national economy.

Typically, those facilities with the highest scores are required to conduct full SVAs, while the lowest scoring facilities may be permitted to perform a simpler, modified vulnerability assessment. The sample system used to assign risk level based on the SRI (Table 3-1) is shown in Table 3-2.

Table 3-2: Security Risk Index

← More Risk							Less Risk →		
12	11	10	9	8	7	6	5	4	3

3.3 Assessing Consequences

DHS defines consequence as the effect of an event, incident, or occurrence. Consequence commonly includes four components: human, economic, mission, and psychological, but may also include other factors. The following is a discussion of how consequence is evaluated in a number of important regulatory and voluntary programs.

3.3.1 CFATS

CFATS Appendix A identifies more than 300 chemicals of interest (COI) and their corresponding STQ based on the consequences associated with one or more of the following three security issues:

1. Release: Toxic, flammable, or explosive chemicals that have the potential to create significant adverse consequences for human life if intentionally released or detonated;

2. Theft/Diversion: Chemicals that have the potential, if stolen or diverted, to be easily used or effectively converted into weapons; and

3. Sabotage/Contamination: Chemicals that, if mixed with other readily available materials, have the potential to create significant adverse consequences for human life.

CFATS Appendix A specifies the chemicals that, if possessed in amounts that exceed or meet the STQ, have the potential to create significant adverse consequences for human life, given the security issues listed above. In the CSAT Top-Screen, the facility must answer questions about the quantity, location, phase, and concentration of any of the COI onsite within a specified time frame. A worst case consequence release scenario must be calculated for those COIs having a release-based security issue to determine the distance from the facility that might be impacted by a release of the COI. The facility must complete an SVA if DHS determines that the worst case consequences reach a level at which the facility is preliminarily considered to be high risk. Consequence is also considered by DHS as a part of the review of an SVA.

3.3.2 MTSA

When conducting an FSA, a Facility Security Officer must analyze the facility background information and the on-scene survey for the likely consequences of an attack on the facility in terms of loss of life, damage to property, and economic disruption. Several methods for assessing consequence developed by the private sector are accepted as compliant with the regulation. (A general description of these methods is described below in Section 3.3.3 and Appendix 8.)

At the port level, the COTP and other port stakeholders utilize the MSRAM to assess consequence in the maritime domain. The consequence of attack scenarios comprises two parts: primary consequence and secondary economic impact. Primary consequences include deaths and injuries, primary economic impacts, environmental impacts, national security impacts, and symbolic impacts. MSRAM also considers consequence mitigation factors including local response capabilities, operational redundancies, and recoverability. Based on this information, the facility is given an overall consequence score.

3.3.3 Private Sector Methods

Private sector methods typically address consequence in terms of features that make a site attractive for an attack. Factors that can mitigate or exacerbate a release are considered, as are proximity to significant landmarks and features, other types of facilities, and various population centers.

Many private sector models assume the Center for Chemical Process Safety (CCPS) definition of security-related worst case consequences, including the potential failure of existing safety and security measures.[13] The worst case in a security context is defined as the potential for chemical release of multiple containers simultaneously versus the failure of a single container. The consequence analysis of chemical releases includes quantifying the size of a release, dispersion of vapor clouds to an end-point concentration, outcomes for various explosions and fires, and the effect of the release on people and structures.

3.3.4 Voluntary Chemical Assessment Tool (VCAT)

VCAT guides a chemical facility owner or operator through the tool in order to prioritize each of the selected assets via an interactive consequence matrix. The consequence matrix uses two primary qualitative factors: (1) the criticality of the loss of the asset and (2) the attractiveness of the asset. The criticality of the loss of the asset considers the loss of life, severe injuries, loss of services or core processes, and so forth. The attractiveness of the asset considers the real or perceived value to an adversary based on several factors, including (but not limited to) how recognizable the asset is to the public. Each qualitative assessment of an asset's criticality of loss and attractiveness receives a score. Those assets with a greater criticality of loss and attractiveness yield a higher score, which indicates a higher consequence if the asset is lost or damaged. These scores are then used in the overall risk calculation.

3.4 Assessing Vulnerability

A second factor in determining risk is the assessment of vulnerabilities. Vulnerability is defined by DHS as a physical feature or operation that renders an asset, system, or network susceptible to disruption, destruction, or exploitation.

Chemical facilities use a variety of vulnerability assessment tools and methodologies in accordance with regulations or on a voluntary basis. Many of these assessment tools have been developed or sponsored by DHS in conjunction with industry, while others have been developed and implemented by industry alone.

3.4.1 CFATS

Following DHS analysis of Top-Screen submissions, any facility that is preliminarily determined to be a high-risk facility is notified by DHS of its preliminary tier assignment and the requirement to complete and submit an SVA or, where applicable, an ASP in lieu of an SVA, in accordance with the CFATS regulatory program. DHS created an SVA methodology as part of its suite of CSAT tools to provide a standard format for SVA submissions.

The CSAT SVA tool requires each facility to identify critical physical and cyber assets associated with each COI as indicated by DHS in the facility's formal preliminary tier notification letter. The tool also requires that the facility inventory and describe their security equipment, access control procedures and equipment, and shipping and receiving procedures. The facility is then instructed to evaluate each critical asset and COI combination against a series of specific, prescribed attack scenarios. These attack scenarios are based on security issues outlined by DHS. The facility is asked to consider an adversary's ability to conduct

---

[13] American Institute of Chemical Engineers Center for Chemical Process Safety, *Guidelines for Analyzing and Managing the Security Vulnerabilities of Fixed Chemical Sites*, New York: Wiley, 2003.

a prescribed attack against the listed asset and COI combinations, taking into account a facility's existing security measures that can help mitigate or reduce the likelihood of the success of an attack on that facility. Additionally, the facility is required to provide their value judgment on the effectiveness of emergency response programs.

As a requirement of the SVA, a facility must also include the cyber industrial control systems and cyber business systems that are associated with each critical asset identified and answer security-related questions about each system. Tiered facilities will be expected to satisfy standards that effectively secure a facility's cyber systems from attack or manipulation.

The CSAT SVA informs the Department's final tiering of high-risk facilities. This enables DHS to direct resources toward the highest risk chemical facilities and identify the risk-based performance standards that they must meet under CFATS.

3.4.2 MTSA

Those chemical facilities satisfying the applicable provisions in 33 CFR 105.105 must conduct an FSA and submit an FSP to the USCG. The FSA must include a description of items such as a facility's access control procedures and equipment, security and safety equipment, facility protective measures, and emergency-response procedures and capabilities. The owner or operator must ensure that an on-scene survey of the facility is conducted in order to examine and evaluate existing facility protective measures, procedures, and operations. Finally, the Facility Security Officer analyzes the information and provides recommendations to establish and prioritize the security measures that should be included in the FSP. Some of the factors the analysis must consider include the vulnerabilities found during the on-scene survey, possible security threats, and likely consequences in terms of life, damage to property, and economic disruption.

Once the FSA is completed, a report is generated and submitted with the FSP to the COTP. The FSP must address each vulnerability identified in the FSA, including specific areas outlined in the regulations, and describe security measures for each of the three MARSEC levels. Prior to approval, the COTP visits the facility to confirm that the FSA report encompasses the vulnerabilities of the facility and that the security measures in the FSP are adequate to address those vulnerabilities.

The FSA must be reviewed and validated each time the FSP is submitted for reapproval or revisions. Once an FSP has been approved by the COTP, it is valid for five years from the date of its approval.

Vulnerabilities are also assessed at the port level with MSRAM. MSRAM considers five factors when scoring vulnerability: (1) attack difficulty, (2) facility security provided by owners and operators, (3) port security provided by local law enforcement, (4) port security provided by the USCG, and (5) the ability of the target to withstand an attack. These factors assess the probability that the layered defense strategy in place will successfully interdict and protect the facility against an attack.

3.4.3 Private Sector SVAs

Numerous robust vulnerability assessment tools were developed by private companies and industry associations before the implementation of Federal security regulations and are still being used by chemical facility owners and operators throughout the Chemical Sector.

Most of the SCC member industry associations promote or require, as a condition of membership, Web-based vulnerability assessments that have been tailored to their members' needs. Short descriptions of these SVA tools are listed in Appendix 8.

A number of these assessments have been critically reviewed to verify that the following four key vulnerabilities of concern have been addressed:

1. Loss of containment of hazardous chemicals on the plant site leading to health or environmental impact;

2. Chemical theft or misuse with the intent to cause severe harm at the facility or offsite;

3. Contamination or spoilage of plant products to cause harm; and

4. Degradation of the assets, infrastructure, or business functions of the facility or company through destructive acts.

Many of these assessments also include cyber vulnerability assessments. Some of the risk-based best practices for cybersecurity include the following:

- Using multi-layer, anti-virus software on both gateway and desktop computer systems;

- Testing software patches and updates;

- Separating networks behind secured firewalls;

- Using network countermeasures such as intrusion prevention systems (IPS) and intrusion detection systems (IDS);

- Prohibiting internet access and e-mail access for industrial control systems;

- Conducting background checks on employees responsible for industrial control systems and business systems; and

- Providing cybersecurity awareness and training courses to employees.

The USCG has accepted some of the private sector vulnerability assessments to satisfy the MTSA FSA requirement.

3.4.4 VCAT

VCAT measures vulnerability for a chemical facility by quantifying the presence of appropriate and applicable security measures that limit or reduce the likelihood of a successful attack. For each security measure, an effectiveness metric per threat and critical asset is assigned. In addition, each measure includes multiple weighted metrics that depend on the type of other security measures present. The weighted metrics allow a facility to capture the synergies of interdependent measures.

Leveraging the information about the facility, its security measures, and other information provided by the user, a vulnerability score is produced and used in the overall risk calculation.

3.4.5 DHS Voluntary Vulnerability Assessment Tool for Cybersecurity

Because chemical processes are highly automated, vulnerability assessments should include the vulnerabilities associated with a facility's cyber systems. The SSA has coordinated with NCSD and the SCC to promote the use of a voluntary cybersecurity assessment tool to raise awareness of cybersecurity issues. Participating companies may receive a free, voluntary on-site review of their cybersecurity through the use of the Cyber Security Evaluation Tool (CSET). CSET assesses the policies, plans, and procedures in place to reduce cyber vulnerability and presents options for consideration for managing cyber risk. The tool provides a flexible and scalable assessment for business systems and industrial control systems and utilizes a comprehensive set of cybersecurity recommendations based on available and emerging standards in the control system community. This information is incorporated into the tool and provides an interface for users to systematically retrieve requirements specific to their control and business system network. CSET provides a means to perform and document a self-assessment of the security posture of a control system environment. The most significant vulnerabilities are highlighted, suggesting areas in which owners and operators may invest resources to reduce the risk to cyber assets.

Sector partners would like to continue to encourage and increase the number of voluntary cybersecurity vulnerability assessments performed in the sector. As part of the Comprehensive National Cybersecurity Initiative (CNCI), the CSCSWG established the Incentives Subgroup, which is composed of public and private sector representatives from the CIKR sectors. The Incentives Subgroup identified incentives that could enhance the private sector's cybersecurity posture and made recommendations regarding which incentives might best be implemented. The subgroup also suggested that the Federal Government encourage the broader adoption of cybersecurity practices that have already been demonstrated to be effective, such as those outlined in Section 3.4.3. Sector partners will engage the Incentives Subgroup when a decision is made to enact the recommendations.

3.4.6 Additional Vulnerability Assessment Programs

3.4.6.1 Site Assistance Visits

Site Assistance Visits (SAVs) are conducted through a voluntary program led by Protective Security Advisors (PSAs), or other Federal team leads, in conjunction with subject-matter experts and local law enforcement, to assist CIKR owners and operators in assessing and characterizing vulnerabilities at their respective sites. These visits, which typically last from one to three days, facilitate vulnerability identification and mitigation discussions between government and industry in the field. At the conclusion of the visit, DHS representatives brief the infrastructure owner or operator on identified vulnerabilities and provide a report for the specific facility with suggested protective measures that are being used throughout the sector.

Information and lessons learned during SAVs are used to develop three types of educational reports that can be used by sector owners and operators as a starting point for identifying asset vulnerabilities. The educational reports are Characteristics and Common Vulnerabilities, Potential Indicators of Terrorist Activity, and Protective Measures.

3.4.6.2 Buffer Zone Protection Program

The Buffer Zone Protection Program (BZPP) provides grant funding to first responders for equipment acquisition and planning activities to address gaps and enhance security capabilities. This voluntary program increases first responder capabilities and preparedness by bringing together private sector security personnel and first responders in a collaborative security planning process that enhances the "buffer zone," the area outside a facility that can be used by an adversary to conduct surveillance or launch an attack. A Buffer Zone Plan (BZP) is a strategic document that

- Defines a buffer zone outside the security perimeter of a specific CIKR target in which protective measures can be employed to deter and prevent terrorist surveillance or attacks;
- Identifies specific threats and vulnerabilities associated with the CIKR target type and the buffer zone;
- Recommends corrective measures for application in or related to the buffer zone that will reduce the risk of a successful terrorist attack; and
- Helps define security measures consistent with each level of the Homeland Security Advisory System and disseminates the information to appropriate authorities and emergency responders.

Upon DHS approval of a BZP, funds may be dedicated by States to the local first responders who developed the plan for use to address shortfalls identified in the plan. Through the BZPP, to date, 244 chemical facilities have been assessed and more than $35.7 million in grant funding has been provided to first responders in jurisdictions surrounding the facilities.[14] In addition, in 2006 and 2007, IP conducted Comprehensive Reviews (CRs) on regions with co-located, high-consequence chemical facilities and utilized the Chemical BZPP to provide $25 million in grant funding for protective measures to State and local first responders.

3.5 Assessing Threats

The final variable in the risk equation is threat. For the purpose of calculating risk, the threat of an intentional hazard is generally estimated as the likelihood of an attack based on the intent and capability of the adversary; for other hazards, threat is generally estimated as the likelihood that a hazard will occur.

Most asset owners and operators must rely on threat input from DHS in order to accurately calculate the risk associated with a given asset. To assist in threat and risk determination, the sector-specific agencies work with the DHS HITRAC. HITRAC works

---

[14] Information provided by the NPPD Protective Security Coordination Division, June 2009.

closely with the U.S. Law Enforcement and Intelligence Communities, SCCs, GCCs, key industry associations, and State and local officials to capture and analyze the entire spectrum of threat as it affects each CIKR sector. Every year, HITRAC provides the sector with an unclassified threat profile that is included in the Chemical SAR. The threat profile includes an assessment of the threat from physical and cyber attacks, as well as natural disasters.

HITRAC, through the Office of Intelligence and Analysis (I&A), also provides the sector with a representative who is responsible for the following:

- Evaluating and monitoring current threats to the Chemical Sector;

- Supporting DHS decisionmakers and external customers with immediate analysis as necessary;

- Maintaining situational awareness of the Chemical Sector; and

- Supporting the IP representative's long-term strategic assessment of risks by providing threat information to be integrated with the unique vulnerabilities and consequences associated with an attack on the Chemical Sector.

The I&A Chemical Sector analyst from HITRAC plays a key role in programs developed by the Chemical SSA to share threat information with sector partners. These include the following:

- **Monthly Unclassified Suspicious Activity Conference Calls:** The Chemical SSA hosts monthly conference calls with Chemical Sector asset owners and operators wherein recently reported suspicious activities near chemical facilities are shared, as well as the latest cybersecurity concerns and updates from the NCSD United States Computer Emergency Readiness Team (US-CERT).

- **Biannual Classified Threat Briefings:** The SSA hosts biannual classified threat briefings for cleared representatives of the private sector. At these briefings, various Federal agencies brief the private sector representatives on general and specific physical and cyber threats of concern to the Chemical Sector, as well as information on the overall threat of terrorism to the Nation. The SSA is responsible for sponsoring clearances for chemical security professionals in order that they may attend these briefings.

These types of briefings provide insight to sector partners on the overall threat to the chemical industry and, more specifically, on potential suspicious activity for which chemical facilities, local law enforcement, and others should be aware.

4. Prioritize Infrastructure

It would be virtually impossible to protect every infrastructure or resource against all hazards. Therefore, the Nation's CIKR protective programs and resilience strategies strive to prioritize assets using a risk-based approach that applies where they offer the most benefit for reducing risk (see Figure 4-1).

Figure 4-1: Prioritize Infrastructure

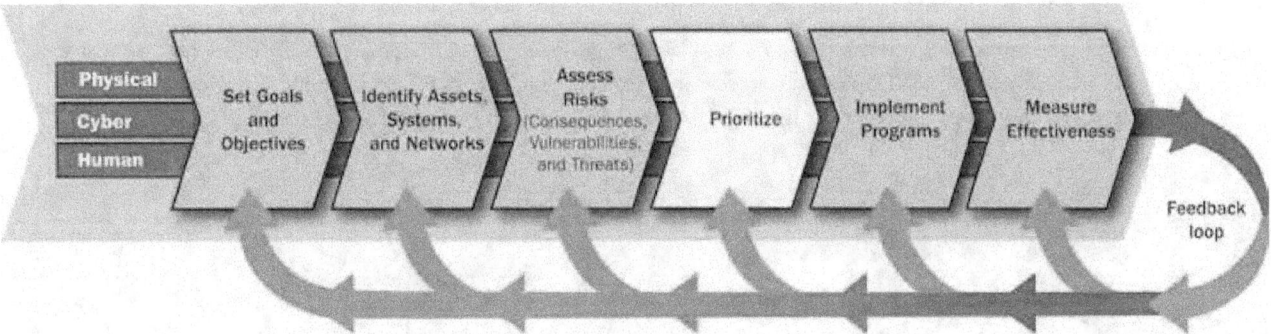

Continuous improvement to enhance protection of CIKR

Within the Chemical Sector, DHS relies on information gathered through regulatory programs, namely CFATS and MTSA, in order to prioritize assets. This chapter addresses the process used to normalize and prioritize the results of assessments of chemical facilities and related systems and networks. The process enables the identification of high-risk assets, systems, and networks both within the Chemical Sector and across other interdependent sectors that are subject to regulations.

4.1 Prioritization Using CFATS

DHS is authorized to identify and regulate the security of chemical facilities that present the greatest security risk. Beginning in early 2008, a consequence-based Top-Screen is required for any facilities that possess an STQ of any chemical of interest listed in CFATS Appendix A. Following DHS analysis of Top-Screen submissions, DHS identifies facilities that are potentially high risk and assigns each facility preliminarily determined to be high risk a preliminary risk tier. Preliminary risk tiers range from Tier 1, representing the highest level of risk, through Tier 4, representing the least risk among the high-risk facilities. Facilities preliminarily determined to be high risk must complete and submit to DHS an SVA. Upon review of the SVA, DHS will provide those facilities still determined to be high risk with a final risk tiering between Tier 1 and Tier 4. Once a facility is notified of its final tier, it will have 120 days to submit a Site Security Plan. The Site Security Plan captures specific security measures that a facility has implemented or will implement to meet the RBPS based on the facility's specific tier and security issues.

Site Security Plans submitted to DHS will be reviewed at DHS headquarters for initial approval; DHS may ask sites to revise their submitted Site Security Plan before it is approved. Following the initial approval of a Site Security Plan, the plan will be verified through an on-site inspection. Facilities will be inspected at regular intervals, with higher risk facilities being inspected first and more frequently. DHS may also inspect a facility at any time based on new information or specific security concerns.

4.2 Prioritization Using MTSA

MTSA regulations require owners and operators of port facilities to conduct an FSA, create a report based on the FSA, and write an FSP. The USCG does not tier facilities except through the expectation that a chemical facility will have more robust security in their FSP as appropriate for the associated risk.

Information submitted as part of an approved FSP is verified by USCG facility inspectors. MTSA regulations require a minimum of two compliance visits to each facility per year, as well as a yearly documented audit of the FSP. Each FSP must be renewed every five years.

4.3 Prioritized Assets and NCIPP

Critical assets identified and prioritized through these regulatory regimes are the primary means through which critical assets are identified for inclusion in the NCIPP. Those assets that meet the consequence-based NCIPP criteria will be included for consideration in the NCIPP Level 1 and Level 2 lists. The NCIPP is explained in greater detail in Section 2.2.3.

5. Develop and Implement Protective Programs and Resilience Strategies

Many Chemical Sector infrastructure owners and operators continue to voluntarily implement protective measures related to the physical, cyber, and human aspects of their individual chemical facilities as part of facility security programs. The SCC works with the Chemical SSA to leverage existing programs while also developing new programs to improve methods for sharing information and to satisfy identified training and technology gaps. The SSA facilitates the identification and implementation of protective programs and resilience strategies by coordinating with sector partners. This chapter of the Sector-Specific Plan describes the processes that the sector partners utilize to implement effective protective programs and resilience strategies across the sector (see Figure 5-1).

Figure 5-1: Develop and Implement Protective Programs and Resilience Strategies

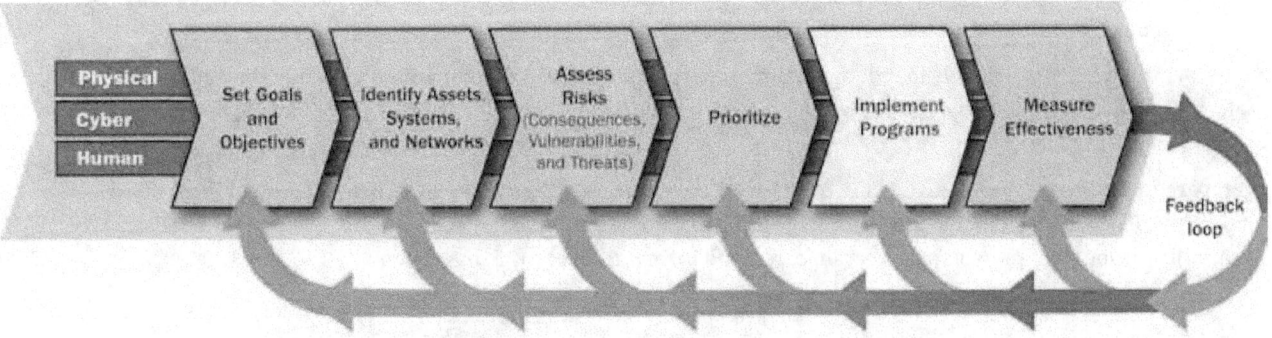

Continuous improvement to enhance protection of CIKR

5.1 Overview of Sector Protective Programs

In the critical infrastructure protection realm, a comprehensive protective program is a coordinated plan of action to strengthen or secure an asset or group of assets by identifying, evaluating, and implementing one or more protective measures or actions. Critical infrastructure protection in the Chemical Sector is composed of a variety of activities that apply pre-incident, during an incident, and post-incident. These activities help to prevent an attack or protect a piece of infrastructure once an incident or attack is underway, as well as mitigate the consequences of and facilitate the recovery from a successfully executed attack or incident. Collectively, this range of activity is often referred to as the "Protective Spectrum" (see Figure 5-2 below).

Protective Spectrum activities common in the sector include the following:

- **Prevention:** Prevention activities are performed in order to increase the likelihood of avoiding an incident or intervening to stop an incident from occurring. These activities focus on deterring and detecting attacks. Examples include heightened inspections, employee background checks, and improved surveillance operations.

Figure 5-2: The Protective Spectrum

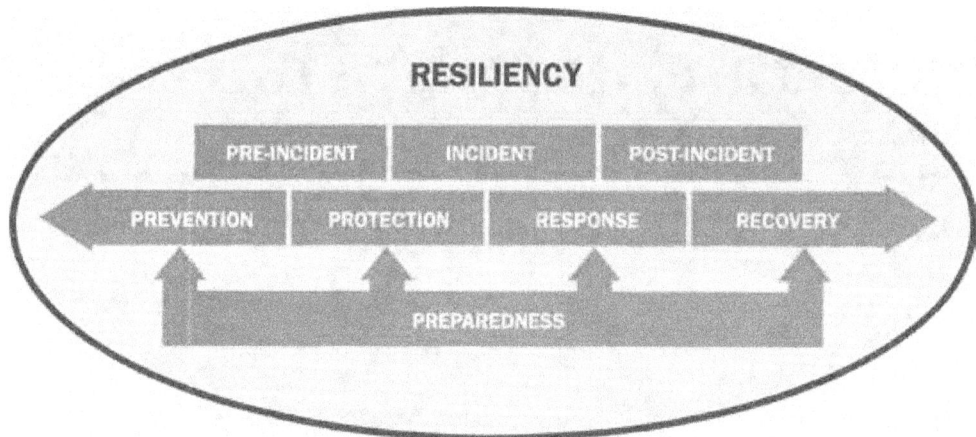

- **Protection:** Protection activities help to strengthen an asset against potential threats or incidents by minimizing vulnerabilities or the potential consequences of an attack or incident. Activities are typically focused on devaluing and defending critical assets that may be targets. Examples include building fences or other barriers, hiring armed guards, installing firewalls to protect cyber assets, and developing redundancies and backup systems.

- **Response:** Response activities allow resources to be called upon during or immediately after an attack to help stop the attack or to mitigate the consequences of the attack. Examples include tactical response plans, mutual-aid plans, and the use of specialized equipment to contain chemical spills.

- **Recovery:** Recovery activities help reduce the time and expense required to return an asset to functionality and normalcy after an incident. Examples include the development of continuity-of-operations plans and the storage of backup or replacement materials offsite.

- **Preparedness:** Preparedness activities are complementary to the other four types of activities found on the Protective Spectrum. They help to develop the elements (e.g., plans, procedures, policies, training, and equipment) necessary to maximize the capability to prevent, protect against, respond to, and recover from an incident.

The NIPP provides the unifying structure for the integration of existing and future public and private sector protection programs and resilience strategies into a single national program. In addition to the NIPP, sector partners are also familiar with several other documents that address CIKR preparedness:

- The National Response Framework (NRF) presents the guiding principles that enable all response partners to prepare for and provide a unified national response to disasters and emergencies and establishes a comprehensive, national, all-hazards approach to domestic incident response; and

- The National Incident Management System (NIMS) establishes standardized incident management processes, protocols, and procedures that all Federal, State, local, and tribal responders use to coordinate and conduct response actions that enhance national preparedness and readiness in responding to and recovering from an incident.

Collectively, these documents have provided a foundation that has enabled sector partners to mitigate risk by fostering a culture of preparedness and resilience through the following actions:

- Developing incident plans that are routinely tested;

- Participating in National Level Exercises;

- Coordinating with first responders during exercises; and

- Developing business continuity plans.

This culture of preparedness was evident in the sector's ability to absorb adverse conditions and successfully recover from hurricanes Ike and Gustav in September 2008, further illustrating Chemical Sector resilience.

Chemical Sector partners develop and implement programs and activities to address all aspects of the Protective Spectrum. The following is a brief discussion of the protective programs and resilience strategies and their role in the sector's overall risk management approach. The programs are divided into regulatory, voluntary, and private sector programs.

5.1.1 Regulatory Programs

The objective of the regulatory programs is to secure the highest risk assets in the sector. As detailed in the previous four chapters, these regulations require high-risk facilities to implement certain measures to decrease their vulnerability to attack. Since the regulatory environment is a dynamic one, facilities that screen into CFATS or MTSA at any point must comply with the security regulations. The next two sections provide additional information on activities that are required of regulated high-risk facilities.

5.1.1.1 CFATS Site Security Plans and Risk-Based Performance Standards

Facilities designated as high-risk chemical facilities subject to CFATS must complete and submit to DHS a Site Security Plan that identifies security measures and processes that satisfy the 18 RBPS developed by DHS for the purposes of CFATS. Table 5-1 lists the 18 CFATS RBPS that identify the areas for which a facility's security posture will be examined. To meet the RBPS, tiered facilities may choose the security programs or processes that they deem appropriate, as long as they achieve the requisite level of performance in each applicable area. DHS has developed a guidance document to describe, in greater detail, each of the RBPS and provide examples of various security measures and practices that a facility may wish to implement to achieve the desired level of performance for each RBPS at each of the four tiers. DHS does not prescribe specific security measures that must be used by any particular site or to meet any particular RBPS.

Table 5-1: CFATS Risk-Based Performance Standards (RBPS)

1	Restrict Area Perimeter
2	Secure Site Assets
3	Screen and Control Access
4	Deter, Detect, and Delay (an Attack)
5	Shipping, Receipt, and Storage
6	Theft or Diversion
7	Sabotage
8	Cyber (Security Measures and Considerations)
9	Response (to Security Incidents)
10	Monitoring

11	Training
12	Personnel Surety
13	Elevated Threats
14	Specific Threats, Vulnerabilities, or Risks (for the Specific Facility)
15	Reporting of Significant Security Incidents
16	Significant Security Incidents and Suspicious Activities
17	Officials and Organizations (Responsible for Security and RBPS Compliance)
18	Records (Security-Related)

5.1.1.2 MTSA Facility Security Plan

Facilities designated as high-risk chemical facilities subject to MTSA must conduct an FSA, create a report based on the FSA, and write an FSP that must address 18 specific security issues (see Table 5-2). These documents are presented to the COTP that has jurisdiction over the chemical port facility for overall FSP approval. The COTP visits the facility to confirm that the FSA report encompasses the vulnerabilities of the facility and that the security measures in the FSP are adequate to address those vulnerabilities prior to approval.

Table 5-2: Sections to Be Addressed in the Facility Security Plan as Required by MTSA

1	Security administration and organization of the facility
2	Personnel training
3	Drills and exercises
4	Records and documentation
5	Responses to a change in the MARSEC level
6	Procedures for interfacing with vessels
7	Declaration of security (for each MARSEC level)
8	Communications
9	Security systems and equipment maintenance
10	Security measures for access control, including designated public access areas
11	Security measures for restricted areas
12	Security measures for handling cargo

13	Security measures for delivery of vessel stores and bunkers
14	Security measures for monitoring
15	Security incident procedures
16	Audits and security plan amendments
17	Facility Security Assessment report
18	Facility vulnerability and security measures summary

5.1.2 Voluntary Programs

The voluntary programs and activities coordinated by the SSA serve one or more of the following functions:

- Information sharing;
- Security awareness;
- Security training; or
- Outreach and education.

The security environment is constantly changing, so it is a primary function of the SSA to share the latest information with sector partners. In addition to monthly suspicious activity conference calls, the SSA, in collaboration with sector partners, has also developed such programs as a Web-based Chemical Security Awareness Training Program, Chemical Sector Explosives Awareness Training, and the VCAT. The objective of these programs is to educate sector partners on current threats and protective measures, and to provide a mechanism to exchange information.

5.1.2.1 Cybersecurity Programs

Recognizing the importance of securing cyber systems in the sector, the Chemical SCC has recently added a representative from the ACC ChemITC Cyber Security Program to act as a liaison with the Federal Government for voluntary partnership activities regarding cybersecurity issues. The SSA, in partnership with the ACC ChemITC Cyber Security Program, works closely with DHS NCSD to exchange information on cybersecurity concerns and to participate in government-sponsored partnership programs, including the following:

- The Cross-Sector Cyber Security Working Group (CSCSWG);
- The Industrial Control Systems Joint Working Group (ICSJWG); and
- The National Exercise Program, Cyber Storm.

Sector partners have also recently collaborated to develop *The Roadmap to Secure Control Systems in the Chemical Sector*. The roadmap outlines the control system component of the cyber elements of the sector's protection and resilience strategies over the next 10 years (see Section 2.2.5). In order to move forward with voluntary implementation, a Roadmap Implementation Committee will be established to coordinate, identify, track, and resolve roadmap implementation issues. The committee will interface with stakeholders; resolve technical, transition, and program management issues; and act as a monitor and central clearinghouse for the actions and milestones discussed in the roadmap. It may also review proposals, sanction work efforts, provide operational support, and develop future implementation strategies as requested.

> **Case Study: The Resilience of Chemical Sector Cyber Systems**
>
> In March 2008, 11 chemical companies participated in partnership with DHS in Cyber Storm II (CS II). CS II was the second in a series of congressionally mandated exercises that examine the Nation's cybersecurity preparedness and response capabilities.
>
> CS II effectively examined the capabilities of participating organizations to prepare for, protect against, and respond to the potential effects of a cyber attack. The exercise provided an environment in which participants could test strategic decision making and interagency coordination of incident response in accordance with national-level policy and procedures. The exercise also validated information-sharing relationships and communication paths for the collection and dissemination of cyber-incident information.
>
> After CS II, Chemical Sector participants began developing a Cyber Crisis Communication Process. Currently, ChemITC is working to finalize the process for notification of escalating cybersecurity incidents among ACC member companies. ACC has acquired a call-tree capability for the new Cyber Crisis Communication Process for use during both cybersecurity and physical incidents.
>
> In September 2010, ACC's ChemITC will be testing the Cyber Crisis Communication Process alongside the National Cyber Incident Response Plan as part of the CS III exercise. The goals will be to ensure that the plans align and are linked as parallel processes. Additionally, the Chemical SSA will be testing processes for communicating effectively with companies that are not members of ACC's ChemITC during a cyber incident. The exercise will assist sector partners in sustaining a resilient Chemical Sector by effectively sharing information during a cyber incident.

5.1.3 Private Sector Programs

The chemical industry has been very effective at leveraging their successful risk management approach to safety and applying it to facility security. As a key component of this strategy, many of the SCC industry associations support the use of vulnerability assessments and the sharing of industry best practices to improve overall security. In the future, industry associations will be reporting the progress that the sector is making in mitigating risk by participating in the metrics process (see Section 6.1.2.3).

In general, private sector partners collaborate to share industry best practices for security across industries, as well as with DHS. They are able to do this through their industry association representative on the SCC, through participation in industry association security committees, or through information sharing at the annual Chemical Sector Security Summit.

5.2 Determining the Need for Protective Programs and Resilience Strategies

The development of the SSP in 2007 was a critical first step in formalizing a process to consolidate protective efforts in the sector into a cohesive protective program for the sector. The sector developed a process to identify protective program needs and to select the protective programs to be recommended for implementation to satisfy those needs. The specific process used for this effort incorporates the steps enumerated below. Please note that these steps refer to programs that were developed jointly with both private and public sector partners. In addition, chapters 2 through 4 included discussions on regulatory protective programs, steps for implementation, and the processes in place for monitoring implementation. Therefore, regulatory programs will not be discussed in this chapter.

5.2.1 Determine Needs and Identify Gaps

In January 2008, HSPD-22, Domestic Chemical Defense, required DHS, in collaboration with its sector partners, to conduct an inventory of existing initiatives, activities, and programs available to chemical supply chain professionals. An analysis was performed to identify gaps in training areas, guidance documents, and recommended practices to adequately address the security awareness of the individuals responsible for any or all areas of the chemical supply chain. In March 2008, the results were submitted to the White House, demonstrating that all segments were adequately addressed by at least one existing training program, protocol, or guidance document regarding threat awareness.

While the HSPD-22 gap analysis represents the status of the sector at a moment in time, it provides a solid foundation upon which to build. As part of the sector's annual process, the SSA, in collaboration with the SCC, GCC, and other sector partners, compares the sector risk profile prepared by HITRAC with sector priorities, goals, objectives, and existing programs. This process identifies where protective measures may be most needed and what vulnerabilities, consequences, or threats may need to be addressed in the future.

In addition to assessing possible training and information gaps, the SSA also works closely with sector partners to assess possible technology gaps to enhance the protective posture of the sector's CIKR. In December 2003, HSPD-7 established the requirement for a national R&D plan for CIKR protection, which is led by DHS S&T. The Chemical SSA reviews the current R&D initiatives under development at S&T to determine their impact on the Chemical Sector and then works closely with sector partners to review these initiatives, along with sector technology requirements, to identify the gaps between sector technology requirements and current R&D initiatives. This process is discussed in more detail in chapter 7.

5.2.2 Identify Potential Protective Measures and Activities Along the Entire Protective Spectrum

The second step in determining the need for a protective program or resilience strategy is the identification of potential solutions to fill the gaps. Activities along the entire Protective Spectrum (prevention, protection, response, and recovery) are considered in this process. Sector partners are consulted regarding existing programs that might be available to fill a gap. If a program cannot be readily identified by Chemical Sector partners, other sectors are consulted to determine if there is an existing program in another sector that could be leveraged for Chemical Sector use. This process is designed to consider the full range of solution sets available when determining the best approach or combination of approaches to management of a specific CIKR protection issue. For example, the sector has identified a need to raise cybersecurity awareness across the sector, but especially at small- and medium-sized facilities. To fulfill this need, the Chemical Sector has worked in collaboration with NCSD to promote CSET at these facilities. Participating companies receive a free voluntary review of the security of their system networks and a summary of their cybersecurity policies and processes.

Solutions for filling gaps in security training can be directly addressed by sector partners more easily than solutions for filling technology gaps or gaps in technological knowledge. Sector partners work with the S&T community to determine if solutions are currently available or if new initiatives need to be funded to address the technology gap. These and other technology processes are discussed in more detail in chapter 7.

5.3 Protective Program and Resilience Strategy Implementation

After the need for a program and its viability are determined, program objectives and content are developed in collaboration with sector partners and, in some cases, in consultation with additional subject-matter experts. A CIPAC Working Group is often established to ensure that the private sector can be engaged in all phases of program development. During the initial stages of program development, implementation milestones are created that will assist sector partners in successful program development. The Development and Implementation Plan for the VCAT is shown in Table 5-3.

Table 5-3: Implementation Example—VCAT Development

CIPAC Working Group is established to develop objectives and content with tool designers.
Beta version of tool is demonstrated to the SSA and SCC members.
Changes to tool are made based on feedback from sector partners.
Tool is piloted by facility owners and operators who volunteer their time.
Feedback from owners and operators is incorporated to improve the tool.
Tool is demonstrated at the 2009 Chemical Sector Security Summit in preparation for sector-wide use.

The initial version of many Chemical Sector programs or tools is first released via a pilot program for limited sector partner use. The pilot program is designed to solicit feedback to ensure that the program content is accurate, timely, and useful. Based on feedback from the participants in the pilot program, the content is improved or changed. The second version of the program is then introduced to the sector as a whole with the help of the SCC and GCC.

The Chemical SSA also has a number of opportunities to evaluate the possibility of cross-sector participation. As one of the six SSAs within the Executive Management Office (EMO), the Chemical SSA meets with other SSAs in the EMO on a regular basis. These meetings provide the opportunity for the SSAs to introduce or provide updates on their sector programs. If a program has cross-sector potential, the EMO facilitates the expansion of the program across the other SSAs. The Partnership and Outreach Division (POD) is also facilitating cross-sector collaboration through the quarterly meetings of the Education, Training, and Outreach Awareness Working Group. This meeting provides the opportunity for all 18 CIKR sectors to share information about their sector awareness and training activities and provides information and initial discussions about possible cross-sector activities.

As mentioned in Section 5.1, the sector collaborates with NCSD and the ACC ChemITC Cyber Security Program on all cybersecurity issues. Cybersecurity is an important issue for all 18 CIKR sectors, and NCSD has been given the lead to coordinate government efforts with the private sector. NCSD has created several working groups to promote awareness of cybersecurity. The CSCSWG brings the CIKR sectors together to address cybersecurity challenges through the exchange of cross-sector perspectives on common vulnerabilities and protective measures, interdependencies, risk assessment methodologies, and management strategies. The ICSJWG engages the sectors to discuss and address cybersecurity issues that impact industrial control systems. The ACC ChemITC Cyber Security Program and the Chemical SSA are active members of both working groups and regularly update the SCC and GCC on cybersecurity issues.

5.4 Monitoring Program Implementation

The Chemical SSA monitors SSA voluntary program implementation by closely tracking implementation milestones developed early in the process and as discussed in Section 5.3. Each milestone also has a feedback mechanism to evaluate the program to date and provides the mechanism to gather the information needed to improve the programs in the future. Additionally, information about program implementation is presented to the SCC and GCC at regular meetings and to owners and operators in the sector through their industry representatives. The sector uses newsletters sponsored by both public and private sector partners to share program successes.

The processes for evaluating program and strategy effectiveness, communicating successes, and recommending changes relate to the NIPP Metrics Program and are described in more detail in chapter 6. In general, metrics are developed for key programs that are directly related to the program goals. Progress made in relation to program and sector goals are reported on a yearly basis through the Sector Annual Reports.

The sector is very active in monitoring technological advances as well. The SSA works with DHS S&T and other Federal partners to monitor the progress of technology advances and collaborates with the SCC to determine how these technologies may be applied to gaps that the sector has identified. This process is discussed in more detail in chapter 7.

6. Measure Effectiveness

Measuring effectiveness is the last chevron of the NIPP risk management framework and informs the feedback mechanism for ensuring the continuous improvement of national and sector CIKR protection activities (see Figure 6-1). This measurement is the shared responsibility of DHS and its CIKR partners. Through the NIPP Metrics Program, the DHS NIPP Measurement and Reporting Office (MRO) works collaboratively with the 18 sectors and other DHS components to measure and report progress. In addition to improving initiatives, the information gathered helps DHS respond to frequent information requests from Congress, the Government Accountability Office (GAO), and the Office of Management and Budget (OMB).

Figure 6-1: Measuring Effectiveness

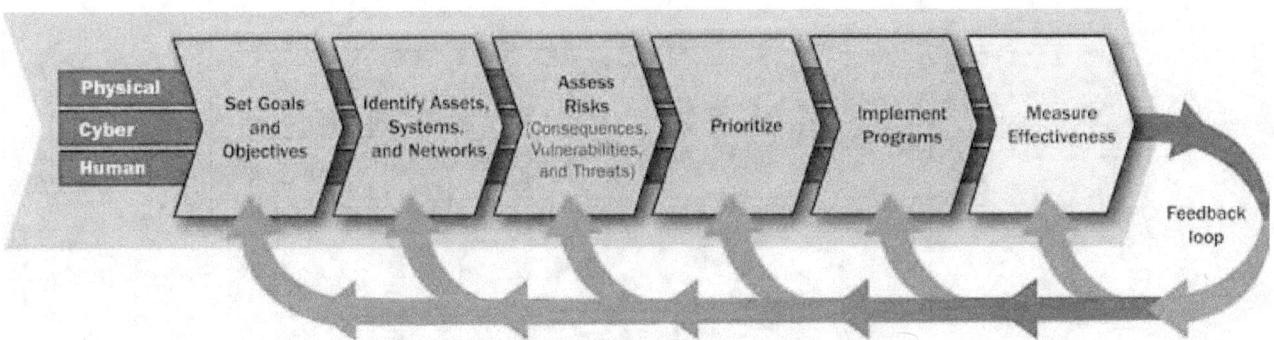

Continuous improvement to enhance protection of CIKR

6.1 Risk Mitigation Activities

The Chemical Sector meets the requirements of the NIPP Metrics Program by identifying Risk Mitigation Activities (RMAs) and selecting those activities that are key to mitigating risk in the sector. Metrics are then developed to measure the progress of the identified key RMAs. This section of the Sector-Specific Plan describes the processes that the sector uses to develop the RMAs that result from the protective programs and resilience strategies.

An RMA, as defined by the NIPP MRO, is a program, tool, initiative, project, major task, or some other undertaking that directly or indirectly leads to a reduction in risk.

The Chemical SSA derives RMAs based on DHS and partner knowledge of sector protective programs and resilience strategies. In 2009, the Chemical Sector referenced more than 60 RMAs in the Chemical SAR, representing individual programs, activities, or tools. The sector anticipates that the list of RMAs will expand over time as DHS's network of partners and knowledge of existing programs in the private sector, academia, and across the government at the Federal, State, local, and territorial levels grows.

All sector RMAs are vital efforts that support the sector's goals and objectives; 11 were identified as key RMAs in 2009. The list of key RMAs is subject to change annually according to a prioritization process. Key RMAs are identified based on the scope of their potential impact (the number of facilities impacted from a security perspective and/or the number of people/facilities likely to adopt an activity) and targeted focus on reducing the specific risks identified in the Chemical Sector SHIRA Profile. The ability of an RMA to reduce risk at high-risk facilities, facilitate information sharing across the sector, and raise awareness of cybersecurity issues is also factored into the prioritization process. The preliminary key RMA prioritization process is depicted in Figure 6-2.

Figure 6-2: Initial Prioritization Process for Key RMA Selection

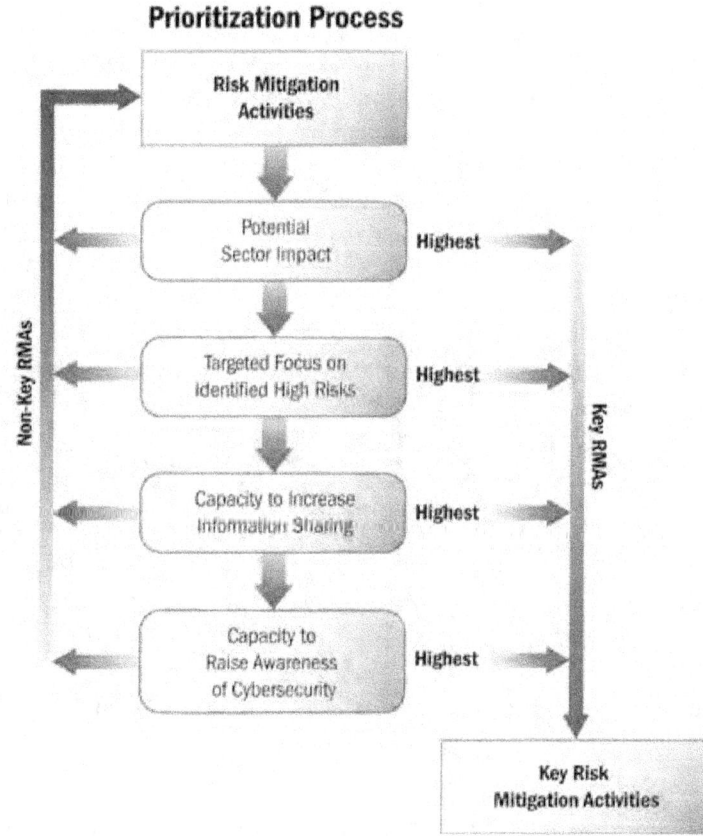

In the first year of key RMA selection, the selection process was completed primarily by the SSA due to time constraints related to changes in the reporting requirements. This initial list of key RMAs for the Chemical Sector can be categorized as regulatory, voluntary, and private sector activities. Each of these categories has a distinct process for metrics development and data collection that relies on the collaboration of sector partners. Over the next several years, the SSA will work with the SCC and GCC to develop a unified approach for the selection of key RMAs and further development of effective metrics.

In addition to the key RMA selection process, the SSA conducts a thorough review of the RMAs alongside sector goals and priorities to ensure adequate alignment. Since Chemical Sector goals were developed using the NIPP risk management framework as a guide, key RMAs also align with the chevrons of the NIPP risk management framework. More detailed information on Chemical Sector RMAs can be found in the 2009 Chemical SAR.

6.2 Process for Measuring Effectiveness

NIPP Metrics are reported in two ways—the National Coordinator Progress Indicators and Sector Progress Indicators, which are described as follows:

- The National Coordinator Progress Indicators describe IP efforts to support NIPP- and Sector-Specific Plan-related activities.

- Sector Progress Indicators collectively describe the progress made by each sector and the effectiveness of different activities within the CIKR sectors.

The National Coordinator Progress Indicators are reported annually in the National Annual Report (NAR). Metrics discussed in the SAR and the 2010 Sector-Specific Plan are considered Chemical Sector Progress Indicators. Metrics can be developed from several different types of data collected as a result of sector activities and include the following:

- **Descriptive Data** provide qualitative information on progress or explain the beneficial value of risk mitigation activities achieved during the reporting period. Examples include TWIC implementation milestones, the feedback provided by Chemical Sector Security Summit participants, and the number of attendees at the biannual classified briefing.

- **Output Data** are used to gauge whether specific activities were performed as planned, to track the progression of a task, or to report on the output of a process. Output data show progress in performing the activities necessary to achieve CIKR protection goals, and they can serve as leading indicators for outcome measures. They also help build a comprehensive picture of CIKR protection status and activities. Examples include the number of TWIC cards issued, the percentage of survey respondents who indicated that they would attend the next Chemical Sector Security Summit, and the number of private Chemical Sector representatives holding a clearance.

- **Outcome Data** are measures that indicate progress, value, or beneficial results toward achieving a strategic goal and associated target rather than level of activity. A high-level metric may demonstrate national achievement of risk mitigation as a result of implementation of a particular CIKR protection initiative. An example might be the number of VCAT users who implemented protective programs based on the tool's assessment of their facility.

The sector uses all three kinds of data and the corresponding metrics that can be developed from the data in order to assess the progress or effectiveness of sector RMAs. The sector is also working toward obtaining outcome data and metrics to assess the progress and effectiveness of key RMAs. Nevertheless, it is expected to be a difficult process due to the challenges listed below.

6.2.1 Process for Measuring Sector Progress

The Chemical Sector faces similar challenges as other CIKR sectors in developing outcome metrics. It is difficult to measure progress toward a strategic goal when the goals are intangible concepts such as mitigating risk or successfully implementing the sector partnership model. Measuring deterrence with an outcome-based measurement program is also difficult because it is driven by a scenario that occurs so infrequently that data are not historically available and may not be available in the future. Therefore, sector partners are concentrating their efforts on activities to reduce the likelihood that an incident will be successful using subjective measures such as successfully conducting vulnerability assessments or testing emergency response plans. Sector partners believe that the protective programs and resilience strategies developed by the sector are effective and successful because the programs and strategies are useful, timely, and are of high quality. In the future, the sector will be developing outcome metrics using agreed-upon program goals and subjective measures such as those mentioned. While some program metrics are yet undefined, owners, operators, and other users of sector programs will be consulted to determine the most appropriate metrics.

The remainder of the discussion in Section 6.2 will be organized around the type or category of key RMA, namely regulatory, voluntary, and private sector. Each category utilizes a slightly different process for measuring effectiveness.

6.2.1.1 Key Regulatory RMAs

As part of the regulatory framework, owners and operators are required to submit information to the Federal entity charged with implementing the regulation. ISCD and the USCG are required under their respective authorities to report progress to the White House, senior leadership, and Congress. While MTSA has been fully operational for some time, CFATS is being implemented through a multi-stage process that is not yet complete. The CFATS RMA may be limited to descriptive or output data initially versus the outcome data that would be available for the MTSA RMA. The SSA will work with ISCD and the USCG to integrate appropriate regulatory metrics into the overall sector metrics.

6.2.1.2 Key Voluntary RMAs

The SSA takes the lead in developing metrics that adequately measure the effectiveness of the key voluntary RMAs. Many voluntary programs are developed with information sharing as a central component of the program. Generally speaking, it is difficult to measure the effectiveness of information-sharing mechanisms.[15] However, the SSA, in cooperation with its sector partners, uses the various types of program data received to routinely assess the following:

- The effectiveness of the information-sharing process, which is determined by whether or not all interested stakeholders are involved and whether or not the information that is shared is disseminated in a timely manner; and

- The quality of the information that is shared, which is determined by considering if the information is useful in assisting facilities reduce risk and increase resilience.

Feedback from our sector partners is necessary in order to collect the information necessary to assess these programs. Feedback mechanisms that are frequently used include participant reviews, creation of working groups, scheduled meetings, and e-mails. The data collected is evaluated and used to improve the content of the program or the way that programs are implemented.

6.2.1.3 Key Private Sector RMAs

The SCC established a CIPAC Metrics Working Group in March 2008 to develop a set of Owner-Operator Metrics that capture the progress that the private sector has made in reducing risk to CIKR. The purpose of Owner-Operator Metrics, as identified by the working group, includes the following:

- Indicating the level of CIKR protection that has been achieved across the sector;

- Demonstrating progress toward enhancing CIKR protection from the perspective of owners and operators;

- Informing public sector efforts and funding decisions toward enhancing sector security; and

- Informing the improvement efforts of owners and operators within the sector.

The working group carefully considered the purpose of the metrics along with key challenges such as data collection, inclusion of the entire risk mitigation continuum (prevention, protection, response, and recovery), and sector diversity. In January 2009, the working group hosted an Owner-Operator Metrics Workshop to gather input from a wider audience. In preparation for the workshop, the working group decided to leverage applicable metrics developed by other sectors, as well as the previous workshop experience of the Energy Sector's ONG Subsector. Subsequent draft metrics were agreed upon at a meeting held March 31, 2009. The individual questions can be grouped into the following five focus areas:

- Risk Assessment;

- Security Planning;

---

[15] The Chemical Sector relies on voluntary participation and sharing of information and there is no mechanism to control or track the information pathway after it has left the SSA. Therefore, the SSA cannot currently measure exactly how much information is shared. Additionally, even if there were a means to measure how much information was shared and with whom, there is no way to isolate the cause (increased information sharing) from the desired outcome (risk reduction).

- Emergency Response Planning;

- Business Continuity Planning; and

- Cybersecurity.

The CIPAC Metrics Working Group will formalize the metrics, develop a method for data collection, report annually (beginning with the 2010 SAR), and continually evaluate and improve the metrics.

Concurrent with the SCC discussion of metrics for physical security, the Chemical Sector also participated in the CSCSWG Metrics Subgroup to develop appropriate metrics to measure the security of cyber systems in all CIKR sectors. The Metrics Subgroup was established to develop cybersecurity progress measures specific to each sector in order to fulfill the metrics requirements under the CNCI. The subgroup identified potential cybersecurity goals, defined generic metrics, assessed the feasibility of each measure, and selected the appropriate sample measures that could be used across several sectors. From these example goals and metrics, the subgroup decided on four generic metrics as a useful starting point for discussion. The SCC, through the CIPAC Metrics Working Group, tailored these metrics for sector use and included them in the Owner-Operator Metrics.

6.2.2 Information Collection and Verification

Metrics data collection is a difficult process in the Chemical Sector. Survey restrictions imposed by the Paperwork Reduction Act constrain the ability of the SSA to collect metrics data from CIKR partners. In addition, there are many other challenges that the sector faces, including lack of a single source or repository for data collection, the complexity and variety of organizations that make up a sector, the cost of the surveys, low response rates to surveys, and companies' concerns in sharing sensitive information on assets or security measures. As described below, the SSA is working to overcome these challenges.

6.2.2.1 Key Regulatory RMAs

DHS, as part of its regulatory authority, collects and verifies security-related information for high-risk facilities subject to CFATS and MTSA regulations. High-risk facilities that must comply with security regulations are also subject to inspection to ensure that the submitted data are accurate. Facilities that are regulated by CFATS will be inspected on a regular basis, but the inspection schedule will be determined by the assigned tier of the facility. Those facilities assigned a higher risk tier may be inspected more frequently than those assigned to a lower tier as outlined in the regulations. Likewise, all MTSA facilities are inspected on an annual basis to ensure compliance with regulations.

The SSA will work with the regulatory authority to facilitate the submission of the appropriate aggregated data for metrics reporting in the SAR.

Refer to Sections 2.2 and 2.3 for a more detailed discussion on how these programs collect and verify the data submitted in accordance with regulations.

6.2.2.2 Key Voluntary RMAs

Collecting appropriate metrics data for voluntary programs is a difficult process for the reasons discussed previously. Program participation is not mandatory nor are follow-up actions required as a requisite for participation. One of the few methods available to the SSA to collect data for metrics is through various feedback mechanisms. These mechanisms include the following:

- Participant surveys;

- Solicitation of program feedback via e-mail; and

- Feedback during informal discussions or meetings, including working groups.

The SSA, in collaboration with sector partners, routinely uses feedback forms to obtain information on the quality of programs, as well as information on improving and expanding current initiatives. The SSA tailors survey templates based on the event and the data needs to ensure accurate and reliable reporting. Sector partners are working to improve feedback mechanisms to collect appropriate information for metrics development.

Another source of data for metrics is Web-based tools such as VCAT. This tool allows owners and operators to identify their facility's current risk level using an all-hazards approach. The tool facilitates a cost-benefit analysis by allowing owners and operators to select the best combination of physical security measures and mitigation strategies to reduce overall risk. All information collected is protected from public disclosure under the PCII Program, but it will be possible to use high-level trending data for metrics reporting.[16]

6.2.2.3 Key Private Sector RMAs

The SCC CIPAC Metrics Working Group is developing a data-collection methodology for Chemical Owner-Operator Metrics. The Metrics Working Group will work with the SCC to determine if the metrics survey questions should be addressed at the facility, company, or association level. Each industry association that is a member of the SCC will be responsible for collecting or possibly aggregating the data for the association that he or she represents. The SCC will then aggregate the data collected from all SCC industry association members and share the data with the Chemical SSA. Only the aggregate data will be included in the SAR.[17]

SCC member associations routinely survey their members for information. Based on the knowledge of their members and their business activities, each association has developed their own process for verifying information that is received and this verification will be reflected in the aggregated data.

6.2.3 Reporting

HSPD-7 requires the Chemical SSA to provide the Secretary of Homeland Security with an annual report on their efforts to identify, prioritize, and coordinate the protection of CIKR. The SARs are due no later than June 1 of each year. The Chemical SSA works in close collaboration with the SCC and GCC to develop this report. Additionally, the SSA works with sector partners to gather the information necessary to measure the level of performance associated with the reported progress indicators and is responsible for entering all data into the NIPP Metrics Portal. Once the SAR is finalized, it is shared with the SCC, GCC, the White House, and Congress.

In addition to the annual reports, the Chemical SSA is asked to provide updated measurement and metrics data on a routine basis to support DHS status reports. This reporting helps DHS measure progress being made under the NIPP and improves the overall national risk management process, while allowing the SSA and sector partners to more effectively coordinate sector-specific RMAs.

---

[16] Owners and operators also have the option of submitting data anonymously.

[17] The final data collection process is discussed in the 2010 Chemical Sector Annual Report.

6.3 Using Metrics for Continuous Improvement

The Chemical Sector Progress Indicators, as part of the larger NIPP metrics effort, provide the mechanism that allows Chemical Sector partners to chart the effectiveness of protection programs and resilience strategies, as well as provide valuable information for future program improvement. Metrics will be reviewed on an annual basis as part of the reporting process to evaluate programs for the following:

- **Quality and type of information that is shared in each program**. This analysis could also help indicate whether the threat environment for the sector is changing and whether future adjustments will need to be considered.

- **Appropriateness of outreach and training programs**. The results of the analysis will help determine if the right people are getting the right information in a usable or actionable form.

- **Gaps in protective programs and resilience strategies**. For those gaps that are identified, new programs may need to be created.

After the evaluation process is completed, results will be used to allocate resources where they can be used most effectively.

By reporting metrics annually, the sector is able to review progress and adapt programs based on the results. For example, data gathered on the Chemical Sector Explosives Threat Awareness Training program (previously called the Vehicle-Borne Improvised Explosive Device (VBIED) Training program) indicated that inconvenient event locations may have contributed to private sector participation rates that were lower than expected. As a result, the location of the training will be changed to enable more private sector participation.

In addition to supporting the evaluation of program progress against sector priorities, metrics serve as a feedback mechanism on other parts of the NIPP risk management framework and on progress toward sector goals. The Chemical Sector's measurement approach promotes continuous improvement by using the data obtained from measurement efforts to inform protective program implementation.

7. CIKR Protection Research and Development

7.1 Overview of Sector Research and Development

Science and technology offer considerable promise in helping to develop efficient and cost-effective ways of mapping potential consequences, identifying potential threats, assessing risk and vulnerability, and enhancing the protective posture of Chemical Sector infrastructure. A focused R&D program will help DHS and its partners enhance the security of the Chemical Sector and achieve the six strategic CIKR protection goals enumerated in chapter 1.

HSPD-7 establishes the requirement for a national R&D plan for CIKR protection. DHS S&T develops this plan in partnership with the White House Office of Science and Technology Policy (OSTP) on approximately the same schedule as the NIPP.[18] This plan is updated annually, typically as an appendix to the National Annual Report. The plan identifies nine technology themes that are applicable to all sectors and specifies three strategic R&D goals as outlined in Table 7-1.

Table 7-1: National Critical Infrastructure Protection R&D Plan

R&D Technology Themes	Strategic R&D Goals
1. Detection and Sensor Systems 2. Protection and Prevention 3. Entry and Access Portals 4. Insider Threats 5. Analysis and Decision Support Systems 6. Response and Recovery Tools 7. New and Emerging Threats and Vulnerabilities 8. Advanced Infrastructure Architectures and Systems Design 9. Human and Social Issues	A. A common operating picture to continuously monitor the health of CIKR. B. A next-generation Internet architecture with designed-in security. C. Resilient, self-diagnosing, and self-healing infrastructure systems.

Within each of these major themes are distinct R&D focus areas. The focus areas have been carefully structured to be complementary, nonrepeating, and supportive of other focus areas wherever possible, with constant consideration of the interrelationship between physical and cyber elements. As part of the sector-specific planning effort, the Chemical SSA has worked with and will continue to work with DHS S&T to identify R&D requirements, initiatives, and gaps that are particularly applicable to the Chemical Sector.

---

[18] The 2004 National CIP (NCIP) R&D Plan is available at **http://www.dhs.gov/xlibrary/assets/ST_2004_NCIP_RD_PlanFINALApr05.pdf.**

The Chemical SSA, SCC, GCC, and other sector partners will work closely to develop a focused R&D program. These sector partners support this effort in a variety of ways, including helping to identify areas where R&D would be beneficial, identifying R&D initiatives currently underway, and sponsoring or actually performing R&D initiatives.

The Chemical SSA strives to remain informed of the R&D efforts of others to share this information with the sector. In order to assist the Chemical SSA in this effort, the SCC formed an R&D Working Group in January 2009. This working group will keep private sector partners informed of the latest developments in the sector's R&D portfolio and will be able to communicate to the Chemical SSA the capability gaps identified by the private sector. The SCC R&D Working Group intends to annually prioritize R&D projects and provide input to the SSA or other customers.

The Chemical Sector acknowledges that there are many cross-cutting R&D efforts, not only within DHS but also in other Federal agencies, academia, and the international arena, for which the chemical industry could be an eventual user of the resulting technology. The sector believes that it is important that these efforts do not duplicate or conflict with one another. Moreover, there should be an emphasis on completing the Chemical Sector's highest priority research first and in a timely manner. In addition, any necessary peer review and dissemination of findings should be available for the sector. The private sector believes that it is important that they be involved in the scoping and technical development of projects, as well as the transition of the work product to the customer. All work products should be accompanied by a clear description of the intended use and the associated limitations of the product, so that new and future uses may be accurately identified. Thus, as appropriate, the Chemical Sector will be involved in the development and review of the Technology Transition Agreement (TTA) document for each project of interest to the sector.

The Chemical Sector's research priorities include, but are not limited to, the following:

- Studying toxicity;
- Tracking toxic chemicals during transport;
- Mitigating chemical releases;
- Developing effective decontamination methods; and
- Reducing the explosive potential of certain chemicals.

The phases of R&D required to bring potential technologies to full maturity and to address one or more security challenges include the following:

- **Basic Research:** The sector looks to the national laboratories and academia to complete 16 long-term basic research projects. DHS S&T utilizes the expertise of nine national laboratories under Section 309 of the Homeland Security Act of 2002. Academia has been directly engaged through a number of activities, ranging from the funding of university-based research centers, such as the DHS S&T Centers of Excellence and Cooperative Centers, to direct funding of specific research programs.

- **Applied Research:** S&T also sponsors applied research and early-stage pilot test and development activities. Applied research is necessary to bring concepts to a level of maturity necessary to transition to the development of a full-fledged set of products or processes. Funding and/or support from the government and private sectors are necessary beyond this point to bring products to a commercially viable state.

- **Short-Term Development:** The objective of these types of initiatives is to design and implement incremental improvements to system/subsystem prototypes that are near operationally ready status. In the past, S&T has sponsored short-term development efforts.

- **Systems Acquisition:** Systems based on technologies that have been proven to work in their final form and under expected or mission conditions can be considered for procurement. This represents the end of R&D and includes developmental tests and evaluations of the system prototype in its intended system configuration to determine if it meets design specifications, or is using the system under operational mission conditions. Systems based on these technologies are candidates for acquisition and deployment.

Figure 7-1: Technology Readiness Levels

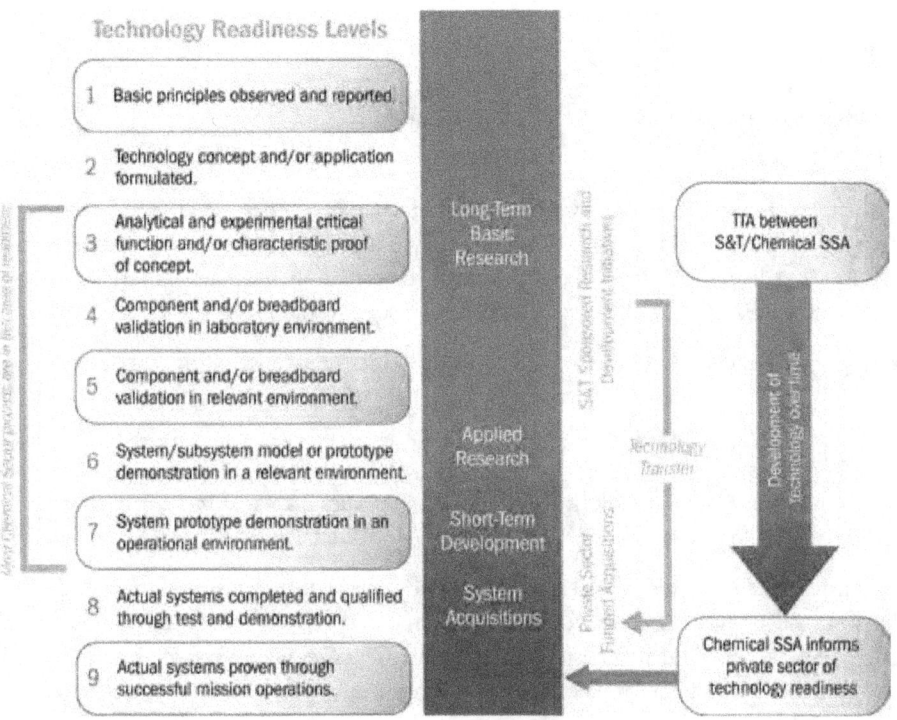

Adapted from an original figure developed by the Transportation Security Administration, which is available in the 2010 Transportation Systems Sector-Specific Plan.

Each technology may require a different path to maturation due to the uniqueness of the technology and the specific requirements. The objective is to allow technologies to develop and mature. During this process, the viability and applicability of each technology is assessed and evaluated. As a result, only those technologies that continue to show promise can be identified, further pursued, and eventually procured.

As shown in Figure 7-1, this progress can be further described using DHS's nine Technology Readiness Levels. This figure also highlights the transition of a technology, which has been proven to be viable and is sufficiently mature, from S&T to the end user.

The Chemical Sector is also interested in applicable IT research. The Roadmap to Secure Control Systems in the Chemical Sector provides a strategic framework for industry and government action toward improving defenses against cyber events that would disrupt operations. The document identifies a requirement for industrial control systems to be secure by design. The Chemical Sector works with the ICSJWG on ICS security issues, including R&D. For more detailed information on the process of roadmap implementation, see chapter 4 of the *Roadmap to Secure Control Systems in the Chemical Sector*.

The Chemical Sector periodically participates with the Institute for Information Infrastructure Protection (I3P) in cybersecurity research. Each I3P research project has a clear focus on useful outcomes—typically security tools, technologies, and practices that can be adopted by companies. Such solutions are made possible by bringing stakeholders and end users into the research process from the start and by integrating technology transfer plans into the project at its earliest stages. More than 100 I3P researchers from dozens of disciplines and backgrounds are collaborating to understand and mitigate critical challenges in the field of cybersecurity. Five multi-institutional I3P teams are currently investigating the following topics:

- Survivability and recovery of process control systems;

- Business rationale for cybersecurity;

- Safeguarding digital identity;

- Human behavior, insider threat, and awareness; and

- Security incentives through risk pricing.

The Chemical Sector participates in a forum hosted by the National Institute of Standards and Technology (NIST) called the Process Control Systems Requirements Forum (PCSRF). This forum is used to identify future requirements for control systems across various CIKR sectors. The Chemical Sector will continue to participate in these forums to take advantage of the opportunity to contribute to improvements in the security of process control system technology.

Chemical Sector research priorities reflect the desire to maintain and increase resilience within the sector.

7.2 Sector R&D Requirements

Annually, through the Chemical SCC R&D Working Group, the sector identifies R&D requirements that have particular benefit to the Chemical Sector. To date, the following priority R&D requirements have been identified:

- **Development of economic models.** In order to assess the economic consequences to the Nation from a terrorist attack, accident, or naturally occurring event on the chemical supply chain, the Chemical Sector needs a model that will calculate the relative risk to the national economy analogous to the human health consequences model. Risk results should be reported both in terms of health impact and economic impact and be as comprehensive as possible to include cradle-to-grave issues.

- **A study on the international dependence and interdependence of the Chemical Sector.** The U.S. chemical industry has seen the erosion of domestic manufacturing capabilities in recent decades. This movement to offshore manufacturing is due to many factors, including additional regulations and their associated costs, increased labor and raw materials costs, and the lack of synergy among multiple regulations that affect the industry's ability to maintain profitability within the United States. The industry needs a study that will help it understand the impacts and repercussions that this trend might have on national security. The study needs to identify the countries with which the United States is developing dependencies regarding chemical supply chain issues and determine the criticality of these dependencies.

- **Better understanding of and updates to the toxicological data being used to determine the hazardous nature of certain chemicals.** Much of the human toxicology data that are currently being used to determine the hazard level of a chemical are dated. The Chemical Sector needs to revisit these data, reexamine their origins, and determine if better data are available, or perform testing and analysis where data are lacking. If toxicology data are going to be used to determine regulatory policy, then it should be based on sound and recent science. The Chemical Sector will work to ensure that the effort includes a plan to obtain reviews from other related agencies (e.g., EPA and OSHA) and to disseminate the newly derived (and properly vetted) information.

- **Analysis and decision support methods that can be used to identify cascading effects of individual or multipoint attacks or natural disasters.** Given the highly interconnected nature of the Nation's infrastructure, attacks on one or more pieces of infrastructure may cause cascading effects that are not easily revealed through the standard consequence assessment. Analysis and decision support systems that help model the cascading effects of attacks on chemical infrastructure, the infrastructure that depends on the Chemical Sector, and the infrastructure on which the Chemical Sector is dependent would help provide more accurate assessment of potential consequences and the more informed allocation of resources.

- **Cyber systems and, in particular, industrial control systems.** Cyber systems are critical and, as such, R&D in this area is of interest. Chemical Sector cybersecurity concerns are very similar to cybersecurity concerns across all 18 sectors and, in particular, the IT Sector. Due to the cross-sector nature of this topic and the expertise of the IT Sector with regard to cybersecurity, the Chemical SSA coordinates with and communicates through the IT GCC and through their R&D Working Group for cyber-related R&D input. For more information on the IT R&D Working Group, see chapter 7 of the IT Sector-Specific Plan.

7.3 Sector R&D Plan

The Chemical SSA continues to develop the Chemical Sector R&D portfolio by closely following the development and progress of existing S&T projects that impact the sector, as well as identifying and submitting capability gaps to the S&T IPT process (see Figure 7-2). The S&T IPT process includes 13 capstone IPTs in different target areas. Even though the Chemical SSA monitors the projects included in most of these IPTs, the Chemical Sector continues to be involved in mainly two S&T Capstone IPTs—Chemical/Biological and Infrastructure Protection.

Figure 7-2: Chemical Sector R&D Coordination With the DHS S&T Process

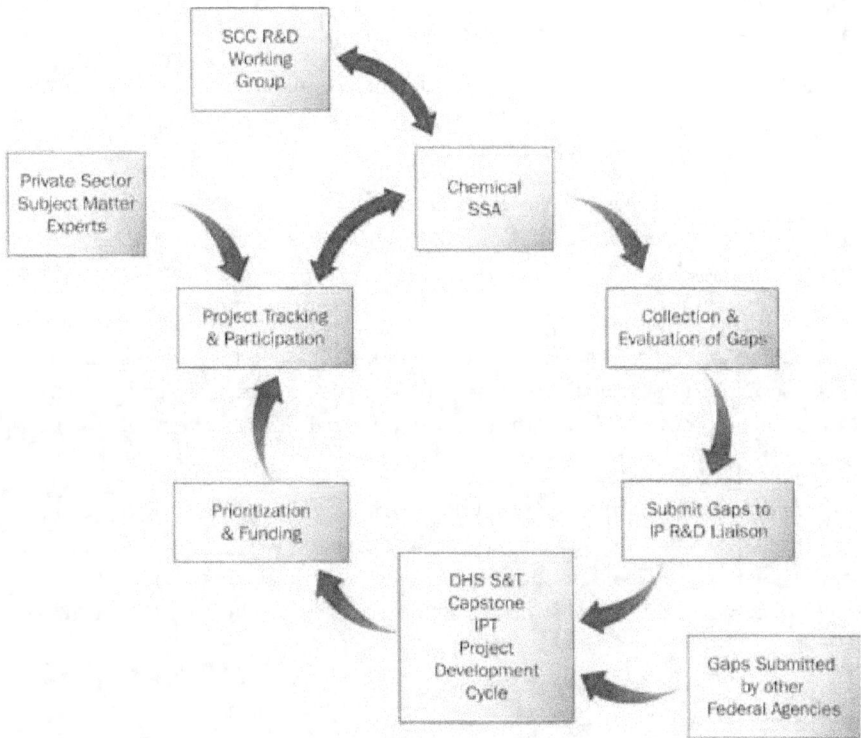

The mission of the Chemical/Biological IPT thrust area is to increase the Nation's preparedness against chemical and biological threats through improved threat awareness, advanced surveillance and detection, and protective countermeasures. This project area contains the bulk of the R&D projects that have a direct impact on the Chemical Sector. Many Chemical Sector partners participate in the technical and review meetings for these projects, providing both data and expertise to the researchers.

As part of developing a more robust R&D plan, Chemical Sector partners will annually review the sector technology requirements against current R&D initiatives to identify gaps. The Chemical Sector R&D Working Group will then work with its sector partners, including industry association members, to prioritize the gaps by significance. A review of the requirements and current initiatives indicates that gaps are likely to exist in the areas of foreign dependencies and toxicology data.

In addition, DHS supports a number of Centers of Excellence that perform targeted research in areas within their particular scope of expertise. The Chemical SSA monitors the research projects being addressed at these Centers of Excellence through participation in the annual project reviews, looking for projects that might be of special interest to some members of the Chemical SCC. If such a research project is identified, it is then included in the list of projects of interest. The Chemical SSA, as well as interested parties within the Chemical Sector, become part of the assessment and review team for these projects.

The SCC and the Chemical SSA coordinate with members of other sectors, such as Transportation Systems, Emergency Services, Water, and Energy, to identify gaps that have cross-sector impact. The development of these cross-sector gaps allows the Chemical Sector to work closely with TSA, EPA, and DOE, among others.

7.4 R&D Management Processes

As part of its SSA responsibilities, the Chemical SSA will take the lead in monitoring sector R&D progress, assessing the impact of R&D efforts on sector goals, and updating this portion of the Sector-Specific Plan. The Chemical SSA will work closely with the SCC R&D Working Group, the GCC, and other sector partners involved in technology R&D that could make Chemical Sector protective programs and resilience strategies more effective or efficient.

The Chemical SSA, SCC, and GCC coordinate with other sectors that share similar technology requirements (e.g., Transportation Systems, Energy, and Water). This group of R&D partners participates in program reviews, project updates, and provides technical advice and data to project researchers.

The Chemical SSA monitors the progress of existing and new R&D initiatives included within the Chemical Sector R&D portfolio and reports to the SCC and GCC on the status of each individual project. The Chemical SSA also ensures that the R&D portfolio as a whole aligns with the goals identified by the sector in the Sector-Specific Plan.

The Chemical Sector operationalizes the results of R&D initiatives by actively participating in the multiple projects within the DHS S&T Chemical/Biological and Infrastructure Protection Capstone IPTs. Sector partners participate on project review panels, work with project researchers to provide the necessary data for project initiatives, and participate in program updates. The results of these research projects inform the sector of potential shifts in chemical risk, transportation issues, and process improvements.

Lastly, sector partners are actively monitoring technology developments by regularly attending conferences and summits where recent developments in technology are discussed. Conferences such as the American Society of Industrial Security and the Chemical Sector Security Summit include trade expositions where vendors are available to discuss technologies that would be applicable to the sector. Sector partners are also able to track the progress of new technologies through trade publications and company Web sites.

8. Managing and Coordinating SSA Responsibilities

This chapter of the Sector-Specific Plan details many of the management and coordination activities that are performed in order for the sector to coordinate protective programs and resilience strategies. Specifically, this section addresses: (1) how DHS manages its SSA responsibilities; (2) how the sector will update and implement the Sector-Specific Plan; (3) resources and budget considerations for sector partners; (4) education, outreach, and awareness strategies for the sector; (5) implementation of the sector partnership model; and (6) how information is shared and protected.

8.1 Program Management Approach

DHS is the SSA for 11 of the 18 CIKR sectors. The Secretary of Homeland Security has designated IP to serve as the SSA for six of the 18 sectors: Chemical, Commercial Facilities, Critical Manufacturing, Dams, Emergency Services, and Nuclear. The SSA EMO is the Federal entity within IP that administers these SSAs.

The Chemical SSA is able to benefit from SSA EMO management of activities that affect all SSAs within this office by maximizing the efficiencies such an organization can provide. These planning and integration activities include the following:

- Managing resources and budgets;
- Hiring personnel to support SSA activities and programs; and
- Managing cross-sector activities and documents.

The SSA EMO has also developed the SSA Project Management Plan (PMP), a comprehensive five-year planning document that describes budget, personnel, acquisition, and programmatic strategies for the six SSAs.

Each SSA within the SSA EMO assumes primary responsibility for sector-specific activities such as the following:

- Developing needed or requested programs and activities in collaboration with sector partners;
- Coordinating information with sector partners;
- Collaborating with sector partners during National Level Exercises (NLEs) or other incidents; and
- Working with the sector to ensure that risk assessment tools are under development or available for sector use.

This chapter discusses each of these areas in more detail and shows how they support the implementation of the SSP and the NIPP risk management framework.

8.2 Processes and Responsibilities

8.2.1 Sector-Specific Plan Maintenance and Update

The Sector-Specific Plan is the primary planning document for the sector, so it is essential that the document reflect substantive changes to sector priorities, goals, processes, and programs. As one of its primary responsibilities, the SSA is accountable for coordinating the development and maintenance of the triennial revision of the Sector-Specific Plan, as well as the annual updates, and ensuring that substantive changes in the sector are reflected in these documents.

The SSA intends that both the annual updates and triennial reviews of the Sector-Specific Plan be iterative and collaborative documents, developed in close partnership with interested stakeholders. The SSA strives to ensure that all appropriate sector partners are provided an opportunity to comment on and review the plan to accurately capture the broad range of interests and initiatives. The SSA works with a dedicated Sector-Specific Plan Working Group composed of SCC members to develop a document that includes the private sector perspective. The SSA also collaborates with Federal agencies on the GCC, representatives from the SLTTGCC, and others, as appropriate, to update and amend the Sector-Specific Plan based on changes to sector priorities, NIPP Program Management Office (PMO) guidance, and regulatory requirements.

The full GCC and SCC, as well as representatives from the SLTTGCC and IP leadership, are asked to review the document and provide substantive input. Comments and changes are adjudicated and revised drafts are issued. The SSA coordinates all comments and maintains full version control over the document. The triennial revisions process also includes final review by the Homeland Security Council's Critical Infrastructure Protection Interagency Policy Committee.

The ongoing objective is to ensure that the revised or updated Sector-Specific Plan is a comprehensive security guidance document that accurately captures the sector landscape, sets forth commonly agreed-upon sector goals and priorities, accurately describes sector protective programs and resilience strategies, and outlines criteria for measuring progress toward risk reduction.

8.2.2 Sector-Specific Plan Implementation Milestones

The Chemical Sector continues to make substantial progress in implementing the NIPP risk management framework using the partnership model. In order to successfully implement the Sector-Specific Plan through the framework, high-level milestones have been developed as shown in Table 8-1. The actions included in the table are shared responsibilities between the SSA and the sector partners, although the SSA is primarily responsible for coordinating with all partners to complete milestones. The milestones will be reviewed annually and updated as needed to ensure continued success in managing sector risk.

Table 8-1: Chemical Sector-Specific Plan Implementation Milestones Aligned With the NIPP Risk Management Framework

Chevron	Milestone
Establish Sector Goals and Objectives	• Collaborate with the SCC and GCC to review sector goals and objectives as part of the annual Sector-Specific Plan review process to ensure that they remain relevant.
Identify Assets, Systems, and Networks	• Continue to ensure that sector partners are informed of CFATS implementation progress. • Participate in the NCIPP and the Critical Foreign Dependencies Initiative on an annual basis.
Assess Risks	• Collaborate with sector partners to ensure that data submitted for the annual SHIRA is accurate. • Promote the Voluntary Chemical Assessment Tool and the Cyber Security Evaluation Tool sector wide.

Chevron	Milestone
Prioritize Infrastructure	• Continue to collaborate with ISCD and to ensure that sector partners are informed of CFATS prioritization deadlines. • Collaborate with sector partners to prioritize key risk mitigation activities and R&D initiatives on an annual basis. • Annually nominate CIKR for the NCIPP Lists.
Develop and Implement Protective Programs and Resilience Strategies	• Continue to collaborate with sector partners to identify training gaps that would benefit from the development of protective programs and resilience strategies in coordination with the development of the Sector Annual Report. • Conduct at least one annual meeting/workshop with relevant sector security partners to identify and submit technology gaps to DHS S&T. • Update the SCC and GCC on sector activities, protective programs, and resilience strategies during regularly scheduled meetings. • Annually review sector-wide programs to ensure that they are relevant and of value to sector partners. • Participate in scheduled National Level Exercises and National Cyber Exercises.
Measure Effectiveness	• Submit metrics data for key risk mitigation activities to the NIPP Measurement and Reporting Office on a yearly basis.

8.2.3 Resources and Budgets

The SSA is responsible for leading the effort to coordinate protective programs and resilience strategies across the sector. However, it is important to note that the private sector and numerous Federal, State, local, tribal, and territorial governments carry out critically important programs in support of the greater CIKR protection mission, based on assessed risk and priorities. In addition to the resources used by the private sector to increase facility security both voluntarily and in accordance with security regulations, the agencies authorized to implement regulations also have substantial budgets. Accordingly, it is beyond the SSA's capability and scope of mission to account for all resources devoted to CIKR protection in the sector, or to direct allocation of those resources. Therefore, this discussion is limited to resources that are administered by the SSA.

Resourcing and budgeting for the six SSAs under the authority of IP are managed through the SSA EMO. The SSA EMO's budget is dedicated exclusively to supporting the mission and functions of the six SSAs under its purview. Using the PMP to guide and prioritize its business processes, SSA EMO works within the IP budget process to submit personnel and program requirements in accordance with the needs of each of the IP SSAs for which it is responsible. As an SSA within the SSA EMO, the Chemical SSA is responsible for outlining SSA personnel needs, budget projections, and sector-specific programmatic priorities in alignment with overarching sector goals, objectives, and priorities. SSA requests are submitted as part of the IP budget, which is incorporated as a component of DHS's annual budget submission to the Office of Management and Budget.

8.2.4 Training and Education

Training, education, and outreach are a key focus of the SSA to enhance CIKR protection capabilities and to successfully implement the NIPP risk management framework. To achieve this, the SSA works collaboratively with sector partners to ensure that programs are developed that complement and build on what is available in the sector or required by regulation.

Many Chemical Sector private sector partners have been proactive in mitigating risks to CIKR. Most of the industry associations within the sector provide their members with guidance documents regarding the development of security plans, as well as industry best practices for CIKR protection. Many of the industry associations also promote or develop risk assessment tools specifically designed for their members (see Appendix 8).

The Chemical SSA works collaboratively with the private sector to build on and expand these efforts, concentrating on those activities that should be promoted to security and risk management professionals throughout the sector. The SSA also works collaboratively with other organizations within DHS to leverage expertise in order to develop and promote these activities. The types of training and education that the sector promotes include the following:

- Web-based tools and other documents to raise general security awareness;

- Web-based risk assessment tools;

- Training and awareness of new or evolving threats and hazards, such as threats from improvised explosive devices;

- General awareness of DHS-sponsored partnership activities that promote CIKR risk mitigation;

- Cybersecurity awareness through working groups and cybersecurity vulnerability assessment tools; and

- Tabletop exercises that test the integrated response of facilities and local first responders to threats or hazards.

In order to foster preparedness and response in the sector, the SSA collaborates with sector partners during National Level Exercises (NLEs). These exercises provide the opportunity for sector partners to test information-sharing processes, incident management procedures, and provide valuable insight into cross-sector dependencies. The lessons learned from the NLE are then incorporated by public and private sector partners into incident management procedures to increase sector preparedness and response in an all-hazards environment.

The sector is also an active participant in NLEs that are focused solely on cybersecurity. These Federally sponsored exercises, known as Cyber Storm, provide the opportunity for sector participants to exercise strategic decisionmaking and interagency coordination of incident responses, and test information-sharing processes for collecting and disseminating cyber incident situational awareness across sectors. Each Cyber Storm builds on lessons learned in order to develop a more sophisticated and challenging incident scenario for the next exercise.

8.3 Implementing the Sector Partnership Model

Chapter 1 included a discussion of the roles and responsibilities of the Chemical Sector CIKR partners who collaborate to mitigate risk in the sector. This section describes the primary mechanisms that the SSA and DHS use to coordinate with key sector partners through the NIPP partnership model. This model is the overarching framework within which the broad CIKR partnership operates.

8.3.1 Chemical Sector Coordinating Council

Throughout the Sector-Specific Plan, it has been stressed that the majority of the assets in the Chemical Sector are privately owned and operated. Consequently, a strong collaboration between DHS and the private sector is necessary to develop a strategy to secure the sector and ensure an efficient integration of the industry's programs into DHS Chemical Sector protection and resilience efforts. The formal means for developing this collaborative partnership was the creation of the Chemical SCC through which the Federal Government can efficiently coordinate Chemical Sector CIKR protection efforts with representatives of a large portion of the sector.

The SCC is composed of a chair and a vice chair, who are owners or operators in the Chemical Sector, and representatives from the following industry associations:

- Agricultural Retailers Association

- American Chemistry Council

- American Coatings Association

- American Petroleum Institute

- Chemical Producers and Distributors Association

- The Chlorine Institute

- Compressed Gas Association

- CropLife America

- The Fertilizer Institute

- Institute of Makers of Explosives

- International Institute of Ammonia Refrigeration

- International Liquid Terminals Association

- National Association of Chemical Distributors

- National Petrochemical Refiners Association

- Society of Chemical Manufacturers and Affiliates

The SCC has regularly scheduled meetings throughout the year and invites the SSA to attend the meetings and update the SCC on sector activities. If an issue or activity requires considerable input from the SCC, a dedicated working group is established to work with the SSA on behalf of the SCC. The working group meets as needed to assist in developing a sector program, staying apprised of the progress of an initiative, to provide valuable feedback on program content, or to review sector documents.

The SCC also provided the means through which the SSA established effective working relationships with owners and operators in the sector. The SSA collaborates with groups of private sector partners when it is beneficial to include their perspective in sector activities, especially during incidents. For example, the SSA regularly communicates with owners and operators to understand the procedures implemented before, during, and after an incident. These conversations have also provided an understanding of some important cross-sector dependencies.

The SCC also has a representative from the ACC ChemITC participating in a nonvoting capacity. This representative updates the SCC on current cybersecurity issues and acts as the Chemical Sector representative on the collaborative working groups that the Federal Government has organized to raise awareness of cybersecurity across all 18 CIKR sectors.

The SCC meets regularly with representatives from across DHS and other Federal agencies to coordinate on CIKR protection issues. During these meetings, the SCC is serving in an operational, rather than an advisory, capacity. To allay concerns that these meetings would be subject to the Federal Advisory Committee Act (FACA), DHS created CIPAC and exempted these meetings from FACA. The annual meetings between the SCC and GCC are conducted as meetings of the CIPAC Chemical Sector Joint Sector Committee.

8.3.2 Government Coordinating Council

The GCC acts as the organizing mechanism through which the SSA coordinates sector CIKR protection activities across the Federal Government, as well as with State, local, tribal, and territorial governments. The Federal departments and agencies who are members of the Chemical Sector GCC include the following:

- Chemical Safety Board

- U.S. Department of Commerce

- U.S. Department of Defense

- U.S. Department of Energy

- U.S. Department of Homeland Security
- U.S. Department of Justice
- U.S. Department of Labor
- U.S. Department of State
- U.S. Department of Transportation
- U.S. Environmental Protection Agency
- Office of the Director of National Intelligence
- SLTTGCC representatives

The SSA, as chair of the GCC, uses the regular meetings to update partners on sector activities, as well as provide the opportunity for sector partners to brief the group on their activities which may impact CIKR protection and resilience in the Chemical Sector. As the SSA becomes aware of cross-sector issues, representatives from other Federal entities are invited to join the GCC. For example, as the SSA expanded outreach efforts to international organizations, DOS was invited to become a member of the GCC and brief the group on their international chemical security programs.

The GCC is also seen as a body of subject-matter experts. The SSA, as a focal point of contact for the Federal Government regarding the Chemical Sector, is often asked to coordinate responses on a wide range of issues in the sector. In order to provide comprehensive responses to submitted inquiries, the SSA confers with GCC members for their specific expertise. For example, the SSA may confer with the EPA representative on issues of chemical toxicity or a representative from the FBI or ATF may be contacted to answer questions on the explosive properties of certain chemicals.

Lastly, the GCC is an effective vehicle for discussing efforts to harmonize security regulations. As mentioned in chapter 1, private sector partners identified the lack of harmonization among the different regulatory authorities as a challenge. Regular GCC meetings provide an opportunity for the implementing agencies to discuss how they can better harmonize the requirements of the different regulations.

8.3.3 State, Local, Tribal, and Territorial Government Coordinating Council

The purpose of the SLTTGCC is to provide a forum for State, local, tribal, and territorial government homeland security directors or equivalents to coordinate with the Federal Government and CIKR owners and operators within the NIPP partnership model. The SSA relies on representatives from this council to provide sector partners with a better understanding of the diverse approaches to homeland security at these various levels of government.

Many State and local governments are interested in chemical facility security and the coordinating councils provide the mechanism to share the latest updates on Federal chemical security legislation. These updates are also important for informing the public sector partners of possible conflicts between Federal legislation and legislation that is proposed or implemented at the State and local levels. GCC meetings are also an important mechanism to obtain State and local perspectives on sector voluntary initiatives. This perspective is especially important for those initiatives that focus on local emergency response capabilities and their coordination efforts with emergency responders at chemical facilities. This topic is also popular with Chemical Sector security professionals attending the annual Chemical Sector Security Summit.

8.3.4 State Chemical Industry Councils

The Chemical SSA engaged State CICs to increase interactions with small- and medium-sized companies. These councils have been an effective mechanism to address security issues at the State and local levels through the Security Seminar and Exercise Series. Representatives from the State CIC and the SSA form a steering group to develop agenda topics and exercise scenarios that the member companies find most relevant and useful. The exercise portion of the program includes a tabletop exercise that simulates a real-world security emergency in order to assess and improve the emergency response and preparedness of owners and operators, State and local law enforcement, and local emergency responders.

8.4 Information Sharing and Protection

8.4.1 Information Sharing

The ability to share information in a timely manner between public and private sector partners is critical to efficient steady-state infrastructure protection activity and to effective incident management. Developing effective information-sharing mechanisms remains a core component of the SSA's critical infrastructure protection and resilience strategy. While the SCC is an efficient mechanism for the SSA and public sector partners to coordinate with private sector representatives, additional means of communication are necessary for information sharing throughout the sector. Communicating with the large number of chemical companies and facilities throughout the Nation is a significant challenge. To reach as many facilities as possible, the SSA utilizes various methods, including collaboration with other Federal agencies, State and local authorities, and the SSA's continued presence at conferences and workshops where homeland security issues are discussed and where members of the Chemical Sector are in attendance.

8.4.1.1 Homeland Security Information Network

The Homeland Security Information Network (HSIN) is the primary information-sharing platform for the Chemical Sector. HSIN users are vetted by the sector to ensure a secure information-sharing environment. HSIN is used by DHS and sector partners to share situational awareness reports, briefing notes from the monthly suspicious activity calls, and for timely updates during and immediately after incidents such as hurricanes. In addition, many of the sector's working groups use HSIN to create dedicated work spaces where information can be posted and shared.

8.4.1.2 Sharing of Threat Information

In response to requests by sector partners, the Chemical SSA hosts activities to share both classified and unclassified threat information. Every month, the SSA hosts a conference call with private sector partners to provide briefings by HITRAC on suspicious activities in the Chemical Sector and a briefing on the current cybersecurity issues by a representative from US-CERT. On a biannual basis, the SSA also hosts a classified threat briefing with appropriately cleared sector partners. These briefings are closely coordinated with the Intelligence Community and are organized to address the concerns of the sector. However, private sector partners have noted that it is still a challenge to share and receive classified information with government officials, especially during incidents.

8.4.1.3 National Infrastructure Coordinating Center

The National Infrastructure Coordinating Center (NICC) serves as IP's focal point for coordination across the 18 CIKR sectors during normal operations, as well as during incidents. During an incident, the NICC provides situation reports to the SSA through the Executive Notification Service (ENS). The SSA, in turn, contacts the SCC and CIKR owners and opera¬tors and related government agencies to develop impact assessments when requested. Owners and operators also inform the NICC when there is suspicious or unusual activity at their facility or when chemicals are unaccounted for during transport. The NICC alerts the SSA for situational awareness or to enlist sector partners to help resolve the situation.

8.4.1.4 Chemical Sector Security Summit

Sector partners have indicated that the Chemical Sector Security Summit is an effective mechanism through which a broad range of the chemical stakeholder community can exchange information and ideas, as well as network with other security and risk management professionals. The summit provides an opportunity for sector partners to ask specific questions about regulatory processes, as well as gain insight into the role of the different agencies and departments involved in the many facets of chemical security. Smaller breakout sessions are organized to address selected topics in detail (e.g., cybersecurity, State and local involvement in chemical security, and freight rail security).

8.4.1.5 Cybersecurity Information Sharing

The Chemical Sector is an active participant in working groups established to raise awareness of cybersecurity issues across all CIKR sectors. Both the SSA and private sector partners attend meetings to stay apprised of the latest information and to provide sector input. Two important working groups are the following:

- **Cross-Sector Cyber Security Working Group:** This working group provides a forum to bring government and the private sector together to collaboratively address cybersecurity risk across all CIKR sectors under the CIPAC framework. The CSCSWG addresses a wide variety of cybersecurity issues and enables comprehensive planning and sharing of information across the community of interested stakeholders. The Chemical Sector was chosen for an information-sharing pilot to explore the processes that the sector uses to share cyber information.

- **Industrial Control Systems Joint Working Group:** This working group is a collaborative effort among the various stakeholders involved in industrial control systems, including participants from the international community, government, academia, the vendor community, owners and operators, and systems integrators. Stakeholders have the opportunity to address efforts of mutual interest, build on existing efforts, reduce redundancies, and contribute to national and international CIKR security efforts. Because of the importance of automated control systems in the sector, Chemical Sector representatives are committed to active involvement in this important NCSD-sponsored cross-sector working group.

8.4.2 Protecting Information

The information used by DHS and its CIKR partners to effectively manage risk and protect the Nation's critical infrastructure may contain sensitive security information or sensitive business and proprietary information. As a result, information protection is a significant concern for the SSA and for CIKR partners who provide this sensitive information. There are a variety of information protection programs that are important to the sector that protect information that is voluntarily shared by sector partners, as well as security information that is collected in order to comply with regulations.

8.4.2.1 Classified Information

Classified information is information that has been determined by a delegated official within the Executive Branch of the Federal Government to require protection because its release or disclosure could cause damage to national security. When a determination is made that information will be classified, it is assigned one of three levels of classification: Top Secret, Secret, or Confidential. The assigned level is based on the potential damage to national security should the information be released. Delegated officials make a determination on classification based on the standards and criteria cited in Executive Order 12958 of March 2003.

8.4.2.2 Chemical-terrorism Vulnerability Information

CFATS created a new category of protected information specific to the Chemical Sector and facilities regulated under CFATS. Chemical-terrorism Vulnerability Information (CVI) was created to protect information about high-risk chemical facilities and their security operations that could be exploited by terrorists, while providing a means to share such information with appropriate security partners.

In Section 550 of the Homeland Security Appropriations Act of 2007, Congress acknowledged DHS's need to both protect and share chemical facility security information. DHS included provisions in the final rule to protect from public disclosure extremely sensitive information that facilities develop for the purposes of complying with CFATS, while at the same time sharing relevant CVI with partners who have a "need to know" CVI in order to carry out chemical facility security activities.

In CFATS, DHS identifies information that constitutes CVI to include the following:

- SVAs;

- Site Security Plans;

- Documents related to the Department's review and approval of SVAs and Site Security Plans, including Letters of Authorization, Letters of Approval, and responses to them;

- Alternative Security Programs;

- Documents related to inspections and audits;

- Records required to be created and maintained by regulated facilities;

- Sensitive portions of orders, notices, or letters;

- Information developed pursuant to the Top-Screen process; and

- Other information designated as CVI by the Secretary of Homeland Security.

Any person with a "need to know," as defined in CFATS, may be granted access to CVI. Before being authorized to access CVI, an individual must complete training to ensure that he or she understands how to comply with the various safeguarding and handling requirements required for possession of CVI. For further information on CVI, see 6 CFR 27.400.

8.4.2.3 Protected Critical Infrastructure Information

Pursuant to the Critical Infrastructure Information Act (CIIA) of 2002, a critical infrastructure information program has been created under which sensitive and proprietary critical infrastructure information submitted to DHS, if it satisfies the requirements of CIIA, will be protected from public disclosure to the maximum extent permitted by law. Data submitted by facility owners and operators through VCAT is an example of the kind of data that would be protected under this program. This program, known as the PCII Program, is being managed by the DHS PCII Program Office within IP. The rules governing the PCII Program are located in 6 CFR Part 29.

8.4.2.4 Sensitive Security Information

SSI is a control designation used by USCG, TSA, and DOT. SSI applies to information related to security programs; vulnerability and threat assessments; screening processes; technical specifications of certain screening equipment and objects used to test screening equipment; and equipment used for communicating security information related to air, land, or maritime transportation. Data submitted by owners and operators in their FSAs and FSPs in fulfillment of MTSA regulations would be protected by this program. The applicable information is spelled out in greater detail in 49 CFR 1520.7.

SSI applies to information that the government obtains from the private sector or develops on its own while carrying out certain security or R&D activities related to any mode of transportation. It protects information that, if disclosed, would be an unwarranted invasion of personal privacy, reveal a trade secret or privileged or confidential commercial or financial information, or make it easier for hostile elements to avoid security controls.

SSI protection pertains to both government officials and Transportations Systems Sector owners and operators with a demonstrated need to know.

8.4.2.5 Sensitive But Unclassified Information or For Official Use Only

For Official Use Only (FOUO) is the marking used by DHS to identify Sensitive But Unclassified information. The unauthorized disclosure of this information could adversely impact a person's privacy or welfare, the conduct of Federal programs, or other operations essential to the national interest and that are not otherwise covered by a statute or regulation.

Other government agencies and international organizations frequently use different terms to identify sensitive information, such as Limited Official Use (LOU); Official Use Only (OUO); and, in some instances, Law Enforcement Sensitive (LES). In most instances, the safeguarding requirements for this type of information are equivalent to FOUO.

At a future date, the designations for Sensitive But Unclassified information may be consolidated under the term Controlled Unclassified Information (CUI). In 2008, the President issued a memorandum to the heads of all Executive Branch departments and agencies that will require the creation of a set of CUI standards that will define the term. However, until the policy standards are developed and published, the terms that are currently in use will remain in effect.

8.4.2.6 Critical Infrastructure Partnership Advisory Council

DHS has exercised its authority under Section 871 of the Homeland Security Act to exempt CIPAC from the Federal Advisory Committee Act.[19] This ensures that CIPAC members can discuss sensitive security issues without the risk that these discussions could become public and jeopardize security. CIPAC can meet as a whole, or in the form of joint committees specific to a particular sector, such as the annual joint meeting of the Chemical SCC and GCC.

---

[19] *Federal Register* (FR) 14930, March 24, 2006.

Appendix 1: List of Acronyms and Abbreviations

ACA	American Coatings Association
ACC	American Chemistry Council
AN	Ammonium Nitrate
API	American Petroleum Institute
ARA	Agricultural Retailers Association
ASP	Alternate Security Program
ATF	Bureau of Alcohol, Tobacco, Firearms, and Explosives
ATSA	Aviation Transportation and Security Act
BZP	Buffer Zone Plan
BZPP	Buffer Zone Protection Program
C	Consequence
Cal ARP	California Accidental Release Prevention
CBP	U.S. Customs and Border Protection
CCC	Chlorine Chemistry Council
CCPS	Center for Chemical Process Safety
CCSC	Coatings Care Security Code
CDC	Certain Dangerous Cargoes or
	Centers for Disease Control and Prevention
CFATS	Chemical Facility Anti-Terrorism Standards
CFDI	Critical Foreign Dependencies Initiative
CFR	Code of Federal Regulations
CGA	Compressed Gas Association
ChemITC	Chemical Information Technology Center
CHEMTREC	Chemical Transportation Emergency Center
CHIRP	Chemical HAZMAT Information Reference Portal

CHLOREP	Chlorine Emergency Plan
CIC	Chemical Industry Council
CII	Critical Infrastructure Information
CIIA	Critical Infrastructure Information Act of 2002
CIKR	Critical Infrastructure and Key Resources
CIPAC	Critical Infrastructure Partnership Advisory Council
CIP CS	Critical Infrastructure Protection Cyber Security Program
CLA	CropLife America
CNCI	Comprehensive National Cybersecurity Initiative
COI	Chemical of Interest
COTP	Captain of the Port
CPDA	Chemical Producers and Distributors Association
CR	Comprehensive Review
CS	Cyber Storm
CSAC	Chemical Security and Analysis Center
CSAT	Chemical Security Assessment Tool
CSB	Chemical Safety Board
CSCSWG	Cross-Sector Cyber Security Working Group
CSET	Cyber Security Evaluation Tool
CSSP	Control Systems Security Program
C–TPAT	Customs–Trade Partnership Against Terrorism
CUI	Controlled Unclassified Information
CVI	Chemical-terrorism Vulnerability Information
CWC	Chemical Weapons Convention
DCS	Distributed Control Systems
DEA	Drug Enforcement Administration
DHS	U.S. Department of Homeland Security
DNI	Director of National Intelligence
DOC	U.S. Department of Commerce
DOD	U.S. Department of Defense
DOE	U.S. Department of Energy
DOJ	U.S. Department of Justice
DOS	U.S. Department of State
DOT	U.S. Department of Transportation
DPA	Defense Production Act

EMO	Executive Management Office
ENS	Emergency Notification System
EPA	U.S. Environmental Protection Agency
EPCRA	Emergency Planning and Community Right-to-Know Act
FACA	Federal Advisory Committees Act
FBI	Federal Bureau of Investigation
FDA	Food and Drug Administration
FMCSA	Federal Motor Carrier Safety Administration
FOUO	For Official Use Only
FSA	Facility Security Assessment
FSLC	Federal Senior Leadership Council
FSP	Facility Security Plan
GAO	Government Accountability Office
GCC	Government Coordinating Council
HAZMAT	Hazardous Materials
HAZWOPER	Hazardous Waste Operations and Emergency Response
HHS	U.S. Department of Health and Human Services
HITRAC	Homeland Infrastructure Threat and Risk Analysis Center
HMTA	Hazardous Materials Transportation Act
HSA	Homeland Security Advisor or Homeland Security Act
HSDN	Homeland Security Data Network
HSIN	Homeland Security Information Network
HSPD	Homeland Security Presidential Directive
HSSM	Highway Security Sensitive Materials
I&A	Office of Intelligence and Analysis
I3P	Institute for Information Infrastructure Protection
IC	Intelligence Community
ICS	Industrial Control Systems
ICS-CERT	Industrial Control Systems Cyber Emergency Response Team
ICSJWG	Industrial Control Systems Joint Working Group
IDS	Intrusion Detection System
IDT	Infrastructure Data Taxonomy
IDW	Infrastructure Data Warehouse
IIAR	International Institute of Ammonia Refrigeration
IICD	Infrastructure Information Collection Division

IICS	Infrastructure Information Collection System
ILTA	International Liquid Terminals Association
IME	Institute of Makers of Explosives
IP	Office of Infrastructure Protection
IPS	Intrusion Prevention System
IPT	Integrated Product Team
ISCD	Infrastructure Security Compliance Division
IST	Inherently Safer Technology
IT	Information Technology
LEPC	Local Emergency Planning Committee
LES	Law Enforcement Sensitive
LNG	Liquefied Natural Gas
LOU	Limited Official Use
MARSEC	Maritime Security
MDE	Maryland Department of the Environment
MRO	Measurement and Reporting Office
MSDS	Material Safety Data Sheet
MSRAM	Maritime Security Risk Assessment Model
MTSA	Maritime Transportation Security Act of 2002
NACD	National Association of Chemical Distributors
NAR	National Annual Report
NCIPP	National Critical Infrastructure Prioritization Program
NCSD	National Cyber Security Division
NIAC	National Infrastructure Advisory Council
NICC	National Infrastructure Coordinating Center
NIMS	National Incident Management System
NIPP	National Infrastructure Protection Plan
NIST	National Institute of Standards and Technology
NLE	National Level Exercise
NPPD	National Protection and Programs Directorate
NPRA	National Petrochemical and Refiners Association
NRC	Nuclear Regulatory Commission
NRF	National Response Framework
NSWC	Naval Surface Warfare Center
OMB	Office of Management and Budget

ONG	Oil and Natural Gas Subsector
OSHA	Occupational Safety and Health Administration
OSTP	Office of Science and Technology Policy
OUO	Official Use Only
P	Probability
PCII	Protected Critical Infrastructure Information
PCIS	Partnership for Critical Infrastructure Security
PCS	Process Control Systems
PCSRF	Process Control Systems Requirements Forum
PHMSA	Pipeline and Hazardous Materials Safety Administration
PMO	Program Management Office
PMP	Project Management Plan
POD	Partnership and Outreach Division
PSA	Protective Security Advisor
PSM	Process Safety Management
R	Risk
R&D	Research and Development
RBPS	Risk-Based Performance Standards
RCCC	Regional Consortium Coordinating Council
RCRA	Resource Conservation and Recovery Act
RCSC	Responsible Care® Security Code
RDP	Responsible Distribution Process^{SM}
RMA	Risk Mitigation Activity
RMP	Risk Management Program
RSSM	Rail Security-Sensitive Material
S&T	Science and Technology Directorate
SAFE	Security and Accountability For Every Port Act
SAR	Sector Annual Report
SARA	Superfund Amendments and Reauthorization Act
SAV	Site Assistance Visit
SCADA	Supervisory Control and Data Acquisition
SCC	Sector Coordinating Council
SERC	State Emergency Response Commission
SHIRA	Strategic Homeland Infrastructure Risk Assessment
SLP-27	Safety Library Publication 27

SLTTGCC	State, Local, Tribal, and Territorial Government Coordinating Council
SOCMA	Society of Chemical Manufacturers and Affiliates
SRI	Security Risk Index
SSA	Sector-Specific Agency
SSA EMO	Sector-Specific Agency Executive Management Office
SSI	Sensitive Security Information
STQ	Screening Threshold Quantity
SVA	Security Vulnerability Assessment
T	Threat
TFI	The Fertilizer Institute
TIH	Toxic Inhalation Hazards (aka toxic-by-inhalation)
TSA	Transportation Security Administration
TSNM	Transportation Sector Network Management
TTA	Technology Transition Agreement
TWIC	Transportation Worker Identification Credential
US-CERT	United States Computer Emergency Readiness Team
USA PATRIOT Act	Uniting and Strengthening America by Providing Appropriate Tools Required to Intercept and Obstruct Terrorism Act
U.S.C.	United States Code
USCG	United States Coast Guard
USDA	U.S. Department of Agriculture
V	Vulnerability
VAM-CF	Vulnerability Assessment Methodology for Chemical Facilities
VBIED	Vehicle-Borne Improvised Explosive Device
VCAT	Voluntary Chemical Assessment Tool
WMD	Weapons of Mass Destruction

Appendix 2: Glossary

Many of the definitions in this Glossary are derived from language enacted in Federal laws and/or included in national plans, including the Homeland Security Act of 2002, the USA PATRIOT Act of 2001, the National Incident Management System, and the National Response Framework. Additional definitions come from the DHS Lexicon, except where otherwise noted.

Asset. A person, structure, facility, information, material, or process that has value. In the context of the NIPP, people are not considered assets.

Chemical Weapon. As defined by the Chemical Weapons Convention (CWC), a chemical weapon is, together or separately: (a) toxic chemicals and their precursors, except where intended for purposes not prohibited under the CWC, as long as the types and quantities are consistent with such purposes; (b) munitions and devices, specifically designed to cause death or other harm through the toxic properties of those toxic chemicals specified in subparagraph (a), which would be released as a result of the employment of such munitions and devices; and (c) any equipment specifically designed for use directly in connection with the employment of munitions and devices specified in subparagraph (b).

Chemical Weapon Precursor. Any chemical reactant that can be used in any stage in the production, by whatever method, of a chemical weapon, including any key component of a binary or multi-component chemical system.

Consequence. The effect of an event, incident, or occurrence. For the purposes of the NIPP, consequences are divided into four main categories: (1) public health and safety, (2) economic, (3) psychological, and (4) governance impacts.

Critical Infrastructure. Systems and assets, whether physical or virtual, so vital that the incapacity or destruction of such may have a debilitating impact on the security, economy, public health or safety, environment, or any combination of these matters, across any Federal, State, regional, territorial, or local jurisdiction.

Critical Infrastructure Information (CII). Information that is not customarily in the public domain and is related to the security of critical infrastructure or protected systems. CII consists of records and information concerning any of the following:

- Actual, potential, or threatened interference with, attack on, compromise of, or incapacitation of critical infrastructure or protected systems by either physical or computer-based attack or other similar conduct (including the misuse of or unauthorized access to all types of communications and data transmission systems) that violates Federal, State, or local law; harms the interstate commerce of the United States; or threatens public health or safety.

- The ability of any critical infrastructure or protected system to resist such interference, compromise, or incapacitation, including any planned or past assessment, projection, or estimate of the vulnerability of critical infrastructure or a protected system, including security testing, risk evaluation thereto, risk management planning, or risk audit.

- Any planned or past operational problem or solution regarding critical infrastructure or protected systems, including repair, recovery, insurance, or continuity, to the extent that it is related to such interference, compromise, or incapacitation.

Cybersecurity. The prevention of damage to, unauthorized use of, or exploitation of, and, if needed, the restoration of electronic information and communications systems and the information contained therein to ensure confidentiality, integrity, and availability. Includes protection and restoration, when needed, of information networks and wireline, wireless, satellite, public safety answering points, and 911 emergency communication systems and control systems.

Dependency. The one-directional reliance of an asset, system, network, or collection thereof, within or across sectors, on input, interaction, or other requirement from other sources in order to function properly.

Function. A service, process, capability, or operation performed by an asset, system, network, or organization.

Government Coordinating Council (GCC). The government counterpart to the Sector Coordinating Council (SCC) for each sector established to enable interagency coordination. The GCC comprises representatives across various levels of government (Federal, State, local, tribal, and territorial) as appropriate to the security and operational landscape of each individual sector.

Hazard. A natural or manmade source or cause of harm or difficulty.

Incident. An occurrence, caused by either human action or natural phenomenon, that may cause harm and may require action. Incidents can include major disasters, emergencies, terrorist attacks, terrorist threats, wild and urban fires, floods, hazardous materials spills, nuclear accidents, aircraft accidents, earthquakes, hurricanes, tornadoes, tropical storms, war-related disasters, public health and medical emergencies, and other occurrences requiring an emergency response.

Industrial Control Systems. The computer-based systems used within many infrastructures and industries to monitor and control sensitive processes and physical functions. These systems typically collect measurement and operational data from the field, process and display the information, and relay control commands to local or remote equipment or human–machine interfaces (operators). Examples of types of control systems include Supervisory Control and Data Acquisition (SCADA) systems, Process Control Systems (PCS), and Distributed Control Systems (DCS).

Infrastructure. The framework of interdependent networks and systems comprising identifiable industries, institutions (including people and procedures), and distribution capabilities that provide a reliable flow of products and services essential to the defense and economic security of the United States, the smooth functioning of government at all levels, and society as a whole. Consistent with the definition in the Homeland Security Act, infrastructures include physical, cyber, and human elements.

Interdependency. The mutually reliant relationship between entities (objects, individuals, or groups). The degree of interdependency does not need to be equal in both directions.

Key Resources. As defined in the Homeland Security Act, key resources are publicly or privately controlled resources that are essential to the minimal operation of the economy and government.

Mitigation. Ongoing and sustained action to reduce the probability of or lessen the impact of an adverse incident.

Network. A group of components that share information or interact with each other in order to perform a function.

Normalize. In the context of the NIPP, the process of transforming risk-related data into comparable units.

Owners and Operators. Those entities responsible for day-to-day operations and investment in a particular asset or system.

Preparedness. Activities necessary to build, sustain, and improve readiness capabilities to prevent, protect against, respond to, and recover from natural or manmade incidents. Preparedness is a continuous process involving efforts at all levels of government and between government and the private sector and nongovernmental organizations to identify threats, determine vulnerabilities, and identify the required resources to prevent, respond to, and recover from major incidents.

Prevention. Actions taken and measures put in place for the continual assessment and readiness of necessary actions to reduce the risk of threats and vulnerabilities, to intervene and stop an occurrence, or to mitigate effects.

Prioritization. In the context of the NIPP, prioritization is the process of using risk assessment results to identify where risk-reduction or mitigation efforts are most needed and subsequently determine which protective actions should be instituted in order to have the greatest effect.

Protection. Actions or measures taken to cover or shield from exposure, injury, or destruction. In the context of the NIPP, protection includes actions to deter the threat, mitigate the vulnerabilities, or minimize the consequences associated with a terrorist attack or other incident. Protection can include a wide range of activities, such as hardening facilities, building resilience and redundancy, incorporating hazard resistance into initial facility design, initiating active or passive countermeasures, installing security systems, promoting workforce surety, training and exercises, and implementing cybersecurity measures, among various others.

Recovery. The development, coordination, and execution of service and site restoration plans for affected communities and the reconstitution of government operations and services through individual, private sector, nongovernmental, and public assistance programs that identify needs and define resources; provide housing and promote restoration; address long-term care and treatment of affected persons; implement additional measures for community restoration; incorporate mitigation measures and techniques, as feasible; evaluate the incident to identify lessons learned; and develop initiatives to mitigate the effects of future incidents.

Resilience. The ability to resist, absorb, recover from, or successfully adapt to adversity or a change in conditions.

The definition recommended by the National Infrastructure Advisory Council is as follows: "The ability to reduce the magnitude or duration of disruptive events. The effectiveness of a resilient infrastructure or enterprise depends upon its ability to anticipate, absorb, adapt to, or rapidly recover from a potentially disruptive event."[20]

Response. Activities that address the short-term, direct effects of an incident, including immediate actions to save lives, protect property, and meet basic human needs. Response also includes the execution of emergency operations plans and incident mitigation activities designed to limit the loss of life, personal injury, property damage, and other unfavorable outcomes. As indicated by the situation, response activities include applying intelligence and other information to lessen the effects or consequences of an incident; increasing security operations; continuing investigations into the nature and source of the threat; ongoing surveillance and testing processes; immunizations, isolation, or quarantine; and specific law enforcement operations aimed at preempting, interdicting, or disrupting illegal activity and apprehending actual perpetrators and bringing them to justice.

Risk. The potential for an unwanted outcome resulting from an incident, event, or occurrence, as determined by its likelihood and the associated consequences.

Risk Management Framework. A planning methodology that outlines the process for setting goals and objectives; identifying assets, systems, and networks; assessing risks; prioritizing and implementing protection programs and resilience strategies; measuring performance; and taking corrective action. Public and private sector entities often include risk management frameworks in their business continuity plans.

Risk Mitigation Activity. A program, tool, initiative, project, major task, or some other undertaking that directly or indirectly leads to a reduction in risk.

Sector. A logical collection of assets, systems, or networks that provide a common function to the economy, government, or society. The NIPP addresses 18 CIKR sectors[21] as defined in HSPD-7.

Sector Coordinating Council (SCC). The private sector counterpart to the GCC, these councils are self-organized, self-run, and self-governed organizations that are representative of a spectrum of key stakeholders within a sector. SCCs serve as the

---

[20] National Infrastructure Advisory Council, *Critical Infrastructure Resilience: Final Report and Recommendations*, September 8, 2009, p. 8. Available for download at **http://www.dhs. gov/xlibrary/assets/niac/niac_critical_infrastructure_resilience.pdf**.

[21] Critical Manufacturing was established as a sector in 2008.

government's principal point of entry into each sector for developing and coordinating a wide range of CIKR protection activities and issues.

Sector Partnership Model. The framework used to promote and facilitate sector and cross-sector planning, coordination, collaboration, and information sharing for CIKR protection involving all levels of government and private sector entities.

Sector-Specific Agency (SSA). Federal departments and agencies identified in HSPD-7 as being responsible for CIKR protection activities in specified CIKR sectors.

Sector-Specific Plan. Augmenting plans that complement and extend the NIPP Base Plan and detail the application of the NIPP framework specific to each CIKR sector. SSPs are developed by the SSAs in close collaboration with other security partners.

System. Any combination of facilities, equipment, personnel, procedures, and communications integrated for a specific purpose.

Terrorism. Premeditated threat or act of violence against noncombatant persons, property, and environmental or economic targets to induce fear, intimidate, coerce, or affect a government, the civilian population, or any segment thereof, in furtherance of political, social, ideological, or religious objectives.

Threat. A natural or manmade occurrence, individual, entity, or action that has or indicates the potential to harm life, information, operations, the environment, and/or property.

Value Proposition. A statement that outlines the national and homeland security interest in protecting the Nation's CIKR and articulates the benefits gained by all CIKR partners through the risk management framework and public-private partnership described in the NIPP.

Vulnerability. A physical feature or operational attribute that renders an entity open to exploitation or susceptible to a given hazard.

Appendix 3: Chemical Sector Profile Based on End Product

To better align with industry self-assessment, the characterization of the Chemical Sector was revised along business lines to reflect current descriptions that are familiar to the chemical industry.[22] Thus, the $689 billion business of chemistry can be divided into five segments: (1) basic chemistry, (2) specialty chemicals, (3) agricultural chemicals, (4) pharmaceuticals, and (5) consumer products. Each of these segments has distinct characteristics, growth dynamics, markets, new developments, and issues. While the boundaries between these segments are not clearly definable, these segments provide a useful way of organizing the thousands of products produced by the Chemical Sector. A breakdown of sector revenue by segment is provided in Figure A3-1. The following are some key characteristics of each segment.

Figure A3-1: Chemical Sector Revenue Comparison by Segment

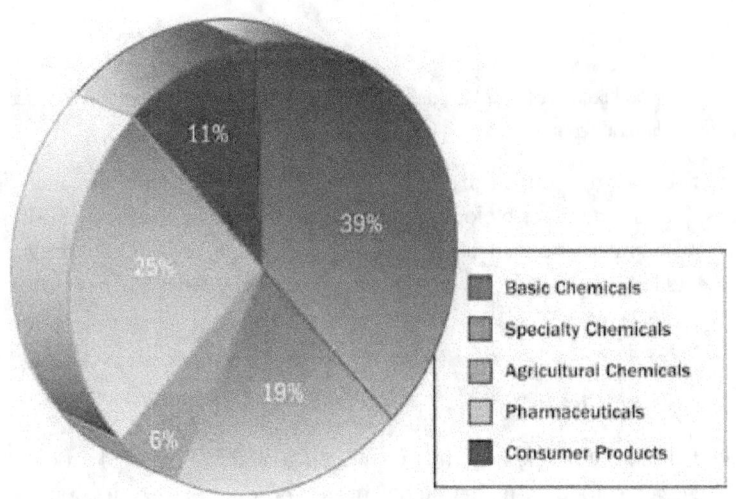

A3.1 Basic Chemicals

Basic chemicals are produced in large volumes, primarily to be incorporated into other manufactured products or to be used as aids in processing. The three main subsegments include the following:

---

[22] American Chemistry Council, 2009 *Guide to the Business of Chemistry*, p. 10.

1. Inorganic chemicals such as sodium chloride, sulfuric acid, lime (calcium oxide), sodium carbonate, and chlorine;

2. Bulk petrochemicals and intermediates such as ethanol, propylene, and ethylene dichloride; and

3. Petrochemical derivatives such as polyvinyl chloride (PVC), polyethylenes, and phenolic resins.

In 2008, basic chemicals generated $267 billion in revenue.

A3.2 Specialty Chemicals

Specialty chemicals are differentiated products manufactured in lower volumes than basic chemicals and are used for a specific purpose, such as a functional ingredient or as processing aids in the manufacture of a diverse range of products. These chemicals enable customers to reduce overall systems costs, enhance product performance, and optimize the manufacturing process through custom-made solutions. That is, they are sold for what they do, rather than for what they contain. Included in this segment are chemicals functioning as adhesives; explosives; catalysts; cosmetic, food, and plastic additives; flavors and fragrances; rubber processing chemicals; and other specialty uses. In 2008, specialty chemicals accounted for approximately $126 billion in revenue.

A3.3 Agricultural Chemicals

This segment is closely related to basic and specialty chemicals. A distinguishing feature is that one end-use customer—farmers—clearly dominates demand patterns. The business includes two major segments: fertilizers and crop protection. In 2008, agricultural chemicals accounted for approximately $42 billion in revenue.

A3.4 Pharmaceuticals

Under the NIPP, the role that pharmaceuticals play in healthcare is addressed in detail in the Healthcare and Public Health SSP. It is described here because those facilities producing pharmaceuticals are part of the Chemical Sector.

Pharmaceuticals include prescription and over-the-counter drugs, in vitro and other diagnostic substances for human or veterinary use, bacterial and viral vaccines, plasma and other biological products for human or veterinary health, and vitamins and other pharmaceutical preparations. This segment also includes biotechnology that cuts across pharmaceuticals and diagnostics with applications in crop seeds, value-added grains, and enzymes, among others. In 2008, pharmaceuticals generated approximately $174 billion in revenue.

A3.5 Consumer Products

Consumer products is actually one of the oldest segments in the business. These are formulated products with a high degree of differentiation, including soap, detergents, toothpaste, hair and skin care products, cosmetics, and perfume, among others. A distinguishing feature is that consumer products are packaged goods. In 2008, these packaged goods generated $76 billion in revenue.

Appendix 4: Chemical Sector Dependencies and Interdependencies

The table below provides further details on the dependencies and interdependencies that exist between the Chemical Sector and the other CIKR sectors. The table is organized alphabetically by sector and is not meant to insinuate a ranking of importance for the listed dependencies and interdependencies.

Table A4-1: Chemical Sector Dependencies, Interdependencies, and Overlaps with Other CIKR Sectors

Sector (SSA)	Dependency/Interdependency/Overlap With the Chemical Sector
Agriculture and Food (U.S. Department of Agriculture [USDA] and the U.S. Department of Health and Human Services [HHS] Food and Drug Administration [FDA])	The Agriculture and Food Sector is dependent on the Chemical Sector for fertilizers, pesticides, and other agricultural chemicals. Many facilities in the Agriculture and Food Sector may also contain sufficiently significant inventories of fertilizers, pesticides, or other chemicals to be considered chemical facilities.
Communications (DHS)	Similar to other sectors, the Chemical Sector depends on the Communications Sector for much of its communications capability. Although an interruption in communications would not necessarily be catastrophic to the Chemical Sector, damage to the Communications Sector can adversely affect the Chemical Sector's ability to communicate with individual facilities, emergency response personnel, and workers repairing utility infrastructure. Under extreme circumstances, the sector's inability to operate may cause some cascading economic impacts. Critical components of the communications industry are made possible by chemical products and thus a disruption at chemical facilities could impact the manufacture of communications components, as well as the ongoing maintenance of these technologies (e.g., cell phones and circuitry).
Critical Manufacturing (DHS)	The Chemical Sector is interdependent with the Critical Manufacturing Sector for certain manufactured industrial goods, including electrical equipment, heavy machinery and transport equipment, and metals for use in chemical products or as catalysts in chemical processes. Many critical manufacturers require chemicals for the production of goods (e.g., chemicals used in the production of metals from ore deposits, and various plastics used in vehicle manufacturing).

Sector (SSA)	Dependency/Interdependency/Overlap With the Chemical Sector
Emergency Services (DHS)	Due to the uniquely hazardous characteristics of certain chemicals, the Chemical Sector has a number of entities that provide emergency response services for incidents involving hazardous chemicals. Examples of these Chemical Sector-specific emergency services include SERCs and LEPCs as required by the Emergency Planning and Community Right-to-Know Act (EPCRA); the U.S. National Response Team; the National Response Center; USCG strike teams; and the EPA regional response teams. Additionally, the Chemical Sector has the Chemical Transportation Emergency Center (CHEMTREC®), an around-the-clock public service hotline for firefighters, law enforcement, and other emergency responders to obtain information and assistance for emergency incidents involving chemicals and hazardous materials. A similar response system, called the Chlorine Emergency Plan (CHLOREP), exists specifically for chlorine-related incidents.
Energy (U.S. Department of Energy [DOE])	The Energy Sector, which consists of two large subsectors—electricity, and oil and natural gas—overlaps with the Chemical Sector primarily as a result of the production of petrochemicals. The Energy Sector has primary responsibility for petroleum refineries and other facilities using and storing petroleum products, many of which also manufacture petrochemicals. The Chemical Sector is dependent on the Energy Sector for critical feedstock such as natural gas and power. An interruption to the power supply would directly affect all chemical facilities located in the affected region. In addition, the interruption could potentially have a cascading effect on other chemical facilities that are dependent on goods or materials provided by the affected facilities. The Energy Sector is dependent on the Chemical Sector for chemical products (explosives) to extract coal or perforate gas and oil wells.
Healthcare and Public Health (HHS)	The Healthcare and Public Health Sector is dependent on the Chemical Sector for many items, including pharmaceuticals, medical devices, medical supplies, and key industrial gases. Therefore, a successful attack on the Chemical Sector could potentially have a cascading effect on the Healthcare and Public Health Sector.
Information Technology (DHS)	The Chemical Sector is interdependent with the IT Sector. Many Chemical Sector facilities rely on IT as a critical component of day-to-day operations, including facility security, as well as a reliance on cyber systems for the secure transportation of chemicals. Additionally, IT is used by DHS and the Chemical Sector to disseminate threat and hazard information. Conversely, the IT Sector is dependent on the Chemical Sector for chemical feedstock in the manufacture of many essential IT hardware items, such as computer chips.
Transportation Systems (DHS, the Transportation Security Administration [TSA], and the United States Coast Guard [USCG])	The Chemical Sector overlaps with, and is dependent on, the Transportation Systems Sector with regard to transporting inbound feedstocks and outbound chemical products. The modes of transportation used to ship chemicals in various stages of the supply chain include ships, barges, trains, trucks, airplanes, and pipelines. Also, transportation assets at facilities occasionally are used to store chemicals. Damage or disruption to the Transportation Systems Sector has the potential to disrupt the movement of raw materials, feedstocks, and downstream chemicals, which can cause cascading effects throughout the Chemical Sector, as well as those sectors serviced by its customers.
Water (EPA)	The Water Sector, which includes drinking water and wastewater systems, is dependent on the Chemical Sector because chemicals are critical for water purification and sanitation. Conversely, many Chemical Sector facilities are dependent on the Water Sector because clean water is essential for many chemical manufacturing processes.

Appendix 5: Authorities

Owners and operators of sector assets are subject to a wide variety of existing authorities and regulations. Of these regulations, two Federal laws, the Chemical Facility Anti-Terrorism Standards (CFATS) (6 CFR 27 et seq.) and the Maritime Transportation Security Act (MTSA) (46 U.S.C. 70101 et seq.), establish direct authority concerning terrorism-related security at Chemical Sector facilities. A considerable number of Federal laws impose safety or other requirements on the production, storage, use, and transportation of chemicals, and these laws indirectly help to secure chemical facilities by requiring restricted access to critical areas; implementation of measures that mitigate the effects of a chemical release; and/or collection and reporting of information concerning chemical production, storage, use, and transportation. Additionally, various States and localities have enacted regulations imposing security requirements on chemical facilities. This appendix sets forth those regulations that are helping to secure the Chemical Sector.[23]

A5.1 Federal Authorities

The paragraphs below outline the authorities vested in different Federal agencies that are related to the security of the Chemical Sector, either directly (e.g., requirements for vulnerability assessments) or indirectly (e.g., risk management planning under the Clean Air Act), and which provide essential support to the DHS in securing the Chemical Sector. The regulations have been divided into those that apply primarily to the security of the manufacturing and storage of chemicals, those that apply primarily to the security of chemicals during their transport and distribution, and those that are focused on securing chemical weapons and monitoring and restricting the use of chemical weapons precursors.

A5.1.1 Authorities Governing the Security of the Manufacturing and Storage of Chemicals

The authorities that most directly impact Chemical Sector activities are those primarily focused on the security of chemicals during the manufacturing and storage of chemicals. HSPD-7 assigns responsibility for managing the security of the Chemical Sector to DHS, and CFATS mandate security standards for high-risk chemical facilities. Additionally, MTSA provides DHS (via the USCG) with regulatory authority over chemical facilities located on or adjacent to bodies of water, and there are multiple other environmental and safety statutes that indirectly help DHS secure the manufacturing and storage of chemicals. These directives and regulations are discussed below.

HSPD-7: Pursuant to paragraph 15 of HSPD-7, DHS has primary responsibility for coordinating protection activities for the Chemical Sector. This responsibility includes managing the implementation of the NIPP risk management framework in the Chemical Sector, as well as working with sector partners to develop and implement this Sector Specific Plan.

---

[23] This appendix is not meant to be a comprehensive list of all regulations that impact Chemical Sector security, but instead simply seeks to identify some of the major regulations along with the corresponding agencies responsible for implementing them.

CFATS: In Section 550 of the Department of Homeland Security Appropriations Act of 2007, Congress gave DHS the authority to require high-risk chemical facilities to complete vulnerability assessments, develop site security plans, and implement the protective measures necessary to meet DHS-defined performance standards. In accordance with this authority, on April 2, 2007, DHS released CFATS as an interim final rule.

Through CFATS, DHS established risk-based performance standards for the security of the Nation's high-risk chemical facilities. CFATS requires covered chemical facilities to prepare Security Vulnerability Assessments (SVAs), which identify facility security vulnerabilities, and to develop and implement Site Security Plans, which include measures that satisfy the CFATS risk-based performance standards. It also allows certain covered chemical facilities, under specified circumstances, to submit Alternate Security Programs (ASPs) in lieu of an SVA, Site Security Plan, or both.

CFATS also contains associated provisions addressing inspections and audits, recordkeeping, and the protection of information that constitutes Chemical-terrorism Vulnerability Information (CVI). Finally, the rule provides the Department with the authority to seek compliance through the issuance of Orders, including Orders Assessing Civil Penalty and Orders for the Cessation of Operations.

MTSA: Under MTSA (46 U.S.C. 70101 et seq.), the USCG has authority over the transportation of bulk and packaged chemicals via water, as well as authority over the security of chemical facilities adjacent to navigable waters that may be involved in transportation security incidents. This authority includes the collection and maintenance of essential infrastructure information concerning these facilities, and review and approval of facility security assessments (FSAs) and facility security plans (FSPs).

Under MTSA, the USCG is to establish area maritime security committees and prepare area maritime security plans for maritime security (33 CFR 102 and 103), which require assessments of ports, vessels, and U.S. facilities to identify those that pose a high risk of being involved in a transportation security incident. Additionally, MTSA requires owners and operators of chemical facilities located contiguous to waterways to complete FSAs and submit FSPs to the USCG for review and approval (33 CFR 105). FSPs must include security measures; procedures for responding to security threats; and detailed preparedness, prevention, and response activities for each maritime security (MARSEC) level. High-risk vessels must also submit security assessments and security plans (33 CFR 104). The USCG also ensures that foreign flag vessels meet certain security standards (33 CFR 104.105(c)).

- **Transportation Worker Identification Credential:** Transportation Worker Identification Credentials (TWICs) are tamper-resistant biometric credentials issued to workers who require unescorted access to secure areas of MTSA-regulated ports, vessels, outer continental shelf facilities, and all credentialed merchant mariners. To obtain a TWIC, an individual must provide biographic and biometric information such as fingerprints, sit for a digital photograph, and successfully pass a security threat assessment conducted by TSA. TWIC was developed in accordance with the legislative provisions of MTSA and the Security and Accountability For Every Port Act (SAFE). The USCG is responsible for enforcement of the TWIC regulations in the maritime domain. All workers who require unescorted access to secure areas of maritime facilities and vessels, and all U.S.-credentialed mariners should have been in compliance by April 15, 2009.

- **Transportation Worker Identification Credential—Reader Requirements** has been released for Advance Notice of Proposed Rulemaking. The public comment period for the proposed rule ended May 26, 2009. The rule will provide guidance on the frequency of biometric checks against TWIC stored data. Frequency will be based on the risk posed by the facility as defined by USCG.

Secure Handling of Ammonium Nitrate: In the FY 2008 Omnibus Appropriations Act, Congress amended the Homeland Security Act of 2002 (6 U.S.C. 361 et seq.) by adding Subtitle J, Secure Handling of Ammonium Nitrate (AN). Subtitle J authorizes DHS to regulate the sale and transfer of AN and requires that DHS develop a regulatory program that oversees or requires (1) the registration of AN sellers and AN purchasers with DHS, (2) point-of-sale verification of AN purchasers, (3) recordkeeping requirements for AN sales or transfers, (4) reporting requirements in cases of theft or loss, (5) compliance inspections, (6) guidance materials and informational posters for the benefit of both AN sellers and AN purchasers, and (7) appeals processes. Subtitle J also provides DHS with the authority to levy civil penalties of up to $50,000 per violation of the subsequent regulation.

Executive Order 13416, Strengthening Surface Transportation Security (December 5, 2006): Executive Order 13416 builds on the improvements made in surface transportation security since the September 11th attacks, specifically actions taken under HSPD-7. The Executive Order requires the strengthening of U.S. surface transportation systems by facilitating and implementing a comprehensive, coordinated, and efficient security program. The order sets deadlines for key security activities, including security assessments of each surface transportation mode and an evaluation of the effectiveness and efficiency of current Federal Government surface transportation security initiatives.

A5.1.1.2 U.S. Environmental Protection Agency Authorities

Clean Air Act: Under Section 112(r) of the Clean Air Act (42 U.S.C. 7401–7671q), any facility that stores, processes, uses, or otherwise handles certain regulated substances above specific threshold amounts is required to develop and implement a risk management program and submit to EPA a risk management plan. The plan must provide information on the regulated substances handled at the facility, an assessment of worst case release scenario(s) and alternative release scenario(s), a 5-year accident history of the facility, and information about the chemical accident prevention and emergency response programs at the facility. Facilities regulated under this section of the Clean Air Act must provide updated Risk Management Program (RMP) information every 5 years. The most recent round of 5-year updates was completed in 2009. Additionally, RMP facilities submit updated information when significant changes occur at their facility. These RMPs are a source of information for DHS and help DHS identify Chemical Sector assets and determine which assets potentially are high risk or high consequence, based on the human health impact.[24]

Emergency Planning and Community Right-to-Know Act (EPCRA): Under EPCRA (42 U.S.C. 11001–11050), States are required to establish State emergency response commissions (SERCs), which, in turn, are required to establish local emergency planning committees (LEPCs). LEPCs are to develop local emergency response plans for releases of extremely hazardous substances. Each facility that handles extremely hazardous substances in excess of threshold planning quantities must notify the LEPC and provide it with the information needed to develop the local emergency response plan. Facilities must also report any releases over a specific quantity to the SERC and LEPC. If the facility is required under the Occupational Safety and Health Act of 1970 (29 U.S.C. 651 et seq.) to maintain material safety data sheets (MSDS), the facility must submit an MSDS for each hazardous and extremely hazardous chemical onsite above the threshold quantity or a list of such chemicals, grouped by hazard (e.g., flammable, toxic, etc.), to the LEPC, the SERC, and the local fire department. The facilities must also submit annual inventories of hazardous and extremely hazardous chemicals managed at the facility over specified threshold quantities during the previous year. The information submitted to the LEPC, the SERC, and the local fire department is useful to DHS to identify at-risk facilities and to determine the mitigation measures and response measures necessary for and in place at each facility.

Superfund Amendments and Reauthorization Act of 1986: The passage of the Superfund Amendments and Reauthorization Act tasked the Centers for Disease Control and Prevention (CDC) Agency for Toxic Substances and Disease Registry with the responsibility for environmental public health logistical support in the event of a chemical release. This act broadened CDC's responsibilities in the areas of public health assessments, establishment and maintenance of toxicological databases, information dissemination, and medical education.

The CDC has developed a National Public Health Strategy for Terrorism Preparedness and Response under which it supports the laboratory response network, a consortium of laboratories ready to provide immediate and sustained laboratory testing

---

[24] As discussed in detail in the main body of the SSP, the value of RMP data is somewhat limited for security purposes due to (1) its focus solely on health impacts to the exclusion of economic and other consequences, and (2) the broader criteria used in RMP analysis given its focus on safety, not security.

and communication in the event of public health emergencies involving chemical terrorism. The CDC also has developed a rapid toxic screen to help responders determine what chemical agents were used, who has been exposed, and to what extent. The CDC also supports training for medical toxicologists to provide surge capacity and expert consultation in the event of chemical terrorism.

A5.1.1.3 U.S. Department of Justice Authorities

Controlled Substances Act: Under the Controlled Substances Act (21 U.S.C. 801) and the Controlled Substances Import and Export Act (21 U.S.C. 951), the Drug Enforcement Administration (DEA) has established regulations for the registration and security of 34 controlled essential (List 1) and precursor (List 2) chemicals. Manufacturers and distributors (including importers and exporters) of the 34 identified chemicals must establish controls to guard against theft or diversion, maintain records of all transactions, and report suspicious orders for these chemicals to DEA. DEA evaluates the effectiveness of List 1 facilities' respective physical security, sales, and storage procedures (see 21 CFR 1301 and 1310.02(a) and (b)). This information can help DHS by identifying the status of controls to guard against theft or diversion of certain highly dangerous chemicals.

Federal Explosives Laws (18 U.S.C. Chapter 40): Under the Federal Explosives Laws, the Bureau of Alcohol, Tobacco, Firearms, and Explosives (ATF) licenses manufacturers, dealers, and importers of explosives, and issues permits for users of explosives. Manufacturers, as well as other licensees and permittees, must submit to ATF the names and identifying information of responsible persons and employees, who must then undergo criminal history background checks. Convicted felons, aliens, and other prohibited persons are disqualified from serving as responsible persons in the business or possessing explosives. The Federal Explosives Laws also require all persons, including manufacturers, to comply with the Federal explosives storage requirements that set forth the standards of public safety and security necessary to protect against explosives thefts, accidental explosions, and other safety and security hazards. For example, the magazines must meet certain construction requirements, bullet-proof standards, and table of distances specifications (e.g., explosive materials must be located a safe distance from public highways and inhabited dwellings). Additionally, manufacturers and other regulated entities must submit to ATF onsite inspections, maintain records of all explosives transactions, and report all thefts and losses of explosives. They must submit product samples upon request by ATF.

A5.1.1.4 U.S. Department of Commerce Authorities

Defense Production Act of 1950 (DPA): Under Title I of DPA, as amended (50 U.S.C. App. 2061 et seq.), the President is authorized to require preferential acceptance and performance of contracts or orders supporting certain approved national defense and energy programs, and to allocate materials, services, and facilities in such a manner as to promote these approved programs. The DPA authority has been extended to support emergency preparedness activities under Title VI of the Robert T. Stafford Disaster Relief and Emergency Assistance Act (the Stafford Act), as amended (42 U.S.C. 5195 et seq.). DPA's definition of "national defense" was also amended in the December 2003 reauthorization of DPA (Public Law 108-195) to include critical infrastructure protection and restoration. The President delegated the priorities and allocations authorities of DPA in Executive Order 12919 (June 3, 1994; amended by Executive Order 13286, February 28, 2003).[26] As part of that delegation, the President designated the Secretary of Commerce to administer the Defense Priorities and Allocations System (DPAS) (15 CFR 700). The Secretary of Commerce has delegated authority to the Secretaries of Defense, Energy, and Homeland Security, and to the Administrator of General Services to place, in accordance with the DPAS regulation, priority ratings on contracts or orders necessary or appropriate to promote national defense. DHS may also endorse and forward to the U.S. Department of Commerce for appropriate action, the requests of owners or operators of critical infrastructure to place, in accordance with the DPAS

---

[26] The President has delegated his priorities and allocations authorities to the Secretary of Agriculture with respect to food resources, food resource facilities, and the domestic distribution of farm equipment and commercial fertilizer; to the Secretary of Energy with respect to all forms of energy; to the Secretary of Health and Human Services with respect to health resources; to the Secretary of Transportation with respect to all forms of civil transportation; to the Secretary of Defense with respect to water resources; and to the Secretary of Commerce for all other materials, services, and facilities, including construction materials.

regulation, priority ratings on contracts or orders in support of critical infrastructure protection or restoration-related programs determined by DHS as being necessary or appropriate to promote national defense.

A5.1.1.5 U.S. Department of Labor Authorities

Occupational Safety and Health Act: Pursuant to the Occupational Safety and Health Act (29 U.S.C. 655) and the Clean Air Act, OSHA requires facilities that handle highly hazardous chemicals to institute a program of process safety management (29 CFR 1910.119). These regulations require regulated facilities to conduct a process hazard analysis, develop written operational procedures, investigate incidents involving the release of covered chemicals (including "near misses"), develop emergency action plans, and conduct compliance audits.

A5.1.2 Regulations Impacting the Security of Chemicals During Transportation and Distribution

Transportation is critical to the Chemical Sector as a key part of the chemical industry's value chain. Raw materials must be moved from suppliers to chemical manufacturers. Basic chemicals, intermediaries, and end products must be transported inside chemical facilities, to distributors, and to end users. While the transportation of chemicals within a facility is clearly the facility owner or operator's responsibility, the transportation of chemicals between facilities is primarily the responsibility of the transportation provider. Consequently, what follows is simply a brief summation of some of the relevant HAZMAT transportation laws and regulations. For more detailed discussion of the authorities concerning the transportation of chemicals and other HAZMAT, please see the Transportation Systems Sector-Specific Plan. Similar to DHS, the U.S. Department of Transportation (DOT) has numerous divisions, many of which regulate, in part, the transportation of HAZMAT.

A5.1.2.1 U.S. Department of Transportation Authorities

Hazardous Materials Transportation Act: Under the Hazardous Materials Transportation Act (49 U.S.C. 5101 et seq.), DOT has the authority to promulgate regulations regarding the safe and secure shipment of HAZMAT. Within DOT, this responsibility has been delegated to the Pipeline and Hazardous Materials Safety Administration (PHMSA) with enforcement authority shared by the modal administrations. Pursuant to this authority, PHMSA has established regulations governing the transportation of HAZMAT on public highways, by rail, in aircraft, and in vessels. In general, commercial HAZMAT move by permission of DOT granted through compliance with PHMSA's regulations, which are internationally harmonized to ensure that transportation is not unduly impeded. These regulations cover classification, packaging, emergency communication, training, and modal-specific requirements. Among PHMSA's rules are those that require sellers and transporters of certain types of HAZMAT to develop and implement security plans and conduct security training for employees. Security plans must be based on vulnerability assessments and must address personnel, access, and en route security related to HAZMAT in transportation. PHMSA ensures that the Nation's HAZMAT transportation rules are uniform through its preemptive authority over non-Federal requirements. PHMSA serves as the U.S. authority for HAZMAT transportation safety and security in international forums.

The Federal Motor Carrier Safety Administration (FMCSA) has also been delegated several authorities under the Hazardous Materials Transportation Act. These include the operational aspects of the vehicles used to carry HAZMAT. In addition to routing and safety permits, FMCSA rules prohibit States from issuing, renewing, transferring, or upgrading a commercial driver's license with a HAZMAT endorsement unless TSA has first conducted a fingerprint-based records assessment of the applicant and determined that the applicant does not pose a security risk warranting denial of the HAZMAT endorsement (49 CFR Parts 383 and 384). The FMCSA also requires States to establish a HAZMAT endorsement renewal period of no more than five years to ensure that each holder of a HAZMAT endorsement routinely and uniformly receives a security screening.

Enhancing Rail Transportation Safety and Security: On November 26, 2008 the Pipeline and Hazardous Materials Safety Administration (PHMSA) published a final rule under Docket HM-232E entitled "Hazardous Materials: Enhancing Rail Transportation Safety and Security for Hazardous Materials Shipments" (73 FR 72181). The final rule builds upon and responds to comments received regarding an interim final rule (IFR; 73 FR 20751) issued on April 16, 2008 by PHMSA. Together the rules require that railroads use routes with the fewest overall safety and security risks to transport security-sensitive hazardous materials. The newly established requirements fully comply with the 9/11 Commission Act of 2007 (signed into law on August 3, 2007). The rules were developed in close consultation with the Federal Railroad Administration (FRA) and were based on the TSA definitions for "security-sensitive material" and "high-consequence target." On July 1, 2008, railroads began implementing the various safety and security provisions of the rule and FRA's compliance oversight and enforcement commenced.

Narrowing the List of Materials Subject to Security Plan Requirements: On March 9, 2010 the Federal Register published a final rule under Docket HM-232F entitled "Hazardous Materials: Risk-Based Adjustment of Transportation Security Plan Requirements." As part of its continuing assessment of hazardous materials risk in transportation, PHMSA in consultation with DHS, narrowed the list of materials subject to security plan requirements. The revised list is based on an evaluation of the security risks associated with specific types and quantities of hazardous materials. Besides refining the list of materials with a potential for misuse in a terrorist incident, the final rule also clarifies certain requirements related to security planning, training, and documentation.

Pipeline Safety Act: Through its authority under the Pipeline Safety Act (49 U.S.C. 60101 et seq.), PHMSA is responsible for ensuring the safe, reliable, and environmentally sound operation of the Nation's pipeline transportation system. PHMSA has safety jurisdiction over approximately 1.6 million miles of gas pipelines and an estimated 155,000 miles of hazardous liquid pipelines. Collaboration between PHMSA and DHS on the use of information concerning pipelines entering and leaving chemical facilities is essential to the responsibilities of both agencies.

Motor Carrier Safety Act of 1984: The Motor Carrier Safety Act prohibits the Secretary of Transportation from eliminating or modifying existing motor carrier safety rules pertaining to vehicles transporting hazardous substances unless and until an equivalent or more stringent regulation has been promulgated under the Hazardous Materials Transportation Act. Under this act, FMCSA has issued rules related to parking and attendance of vehicles transporting HAZMAT.

Federal Rail Safety Act: Under authority designated from the Secretary of Transportation, the Federal Railroad Administration's regulatory responsibilities include the safe and secure movement of freight on railways across the United States. This responsibility includes the design, manufacture, and repair of the equipment, freight cars, locomotives, and track used to carry packaged HAZMAT, and the gathering of data on the movement of these chemicals throughout the United States, as well as internationally between the United States, Canada, and Mexico.

A5.1.2.2 DHS Authorities

Rail Transportation Security: The TSA has security requirements (49 CFR 1580) for rail transportation that include freight railroad carriers and rail operations at certain fixed-site facilities that ship or receive specified HAZMAT by rail. The regulation codifies the scope of TSA's existing inspection program, requiring regulated parties to allow TSA and other DHS officials to enter, inspect, and test property, facilities, and records relevant to rail security. This section also requires parties to designate rail security coordinators and report significant security concerns to DHS. Freight rail carriers and certain facilities handling rail security-sensitive materials must also be able to report location and shipping information to TSA upon request and implement chain-of-custody requirements to ensure a positive and secure exchange of rail security-sensitive materials.

Aviation Transportation and Security Act (ATSA) and DHS Delegation Number 7060.2: Under ATSA (Public Law 107-71, 115 Stat. 597) and authority delegated under the Homeland Security Act, Section 403(2), and DHS Delegation Number 7060.2, TSA is responsible for the security of the movement of chemicals in all modes of transportation (49 U.S.C. 114(d)). Such authority addresses one aspect of the chemical industry's value chain—transportation—and should be coordinated with authorities addressing security within chemical facilities, as well as the interface between the facility and transportation assets.

Hazardous Materials Transportation Act (HMTA): HMTA was amended by the USA PATRIOT Act, Public Law 107-56, 115 Stat. 272, Section 1012, and, more recently, the Safe, Accountable, Flexible, Efficient Transportation Equity Act: A Legacy for

Users (SAFETEA-LU), Public Law 109-59 at 49 U.S.C. 5103a to require TSA, in conjunction with DOT, to administer safeguards for licensing HAZMAT transport drivers. Pursuant to this responsibility, TSA published regulations that can be found at 49 CFR Part 1572. Under these rules, the roughly 3.5 million commercial drivers with HAZMAT endorsements on their commercial driver's licenses are required to undergo a periodic security assessment based on a review of FBI criminal records, and immigration and other relevant international databases, as appropriate.

Trade Act of 2002: Section 343(a) of the Trade Act (Public Law 107-210, 116 Stat. 933), as amended by Section 108 of MTSA, requires DHS, through U.S. Customs and Border Protection (CBP), to collect electronic cargo information from all modes of commercial transport prior to the arrival of the cargo in, or its departure from, the United States. The information required must be sufficient to enable CBP to identify high-risk shipments. The regulations enforcing this requirement, 19 CFR Parts 4, 103, 113, 122, 123, 178, and 192, require advance transmission of electronic cargo information to CBP by way of a CBP-approved electronic data interchange system. Such information must include the actual chemical name (not brand name) or the United Nations HAZMAT code identifier number for all shipments of chemicals and HAZMAT. This information assists DHS in tracking the movement of HAZMAT in order to ensure cargo safety and security.

A5.1.2.3 U.S. Department of Justice Authorities

Federal Explosives Laws (18 U.S.C. Chapter 40): 18 U.S.C. 842 makes it unlawful for any person other than a licensee or permittee knowingly to transport, ship, cause to be transported, or receive any explosive materials, or to distribute explosive materials to any person other than a licensee or permittee. ATF issues the licenses and permits. See Section A4.1.1 above for more details. Generally, the transportation aspect of explosives distribution is exempt under 18 U.S.C. 845.

A5.1.3 Authorities Directed at Securing Chemical Weapons and Monitoring and Restricting the Use of Chemical Weapons Precursors

Many chemical facilities do manufacture, use, store, or distribute chemicals with legitimate uses that can also serve as chemical weapons precursors. In light of this fact, DHS requires chemical facilities that are determined to be high risk based on their possession of materials that, if misused, could contribute to the development of chemical weapons, to comply with CFATS (discussed in Section A4.1.1 above). Other regulations regarding the security of chemical weapons and their precursors that may have a direct impact on members of the Chemical Sector are listed below.

A5.1.3.1 U.S. Department of Commerce Authorities

Export Administration Regulations: DOC regulates the export of dual-use items (i.e., items with both commercial and potential military uses), including those covered by the Chemical Weapons Convention (CWC) under the Export Administration Regulations (15 CFR 730 et seq.). DOC also regulates the export of other chemicals, and related equipment and technology of proliferation concern as controlled by the Australia Group.

Chemical Weapons Convention Implementation Act of 1988: The Chemical Weapons Convention (CWC) Implementation Act (22 U.S.C. 6701 et seq.) authorizes the collection of information on defined activities involving certain chemicals covered by the CWC, as well as the hosting of onsite inspections by the Organization for the Prohibition of Chemical Weapons, the organization responsible for administering and verifying CWC compliance worldwide. Executive Order 13128 delegates authority to DOC to promulgate regulations, obtain and execute warrants, provide assistance to certain facilities, and carry out appropriate functions to implement the CWC, consistent with the act. DOC's CWC Regulations (15 CFR 710 et seq.) require facilities involved in CWC-covered activities and chemicals at specific threshold amounts to submit annual declarations and reports, and submit to onsite inspections. The declarations contain information on quantities produced, processed, consumed, exported, and/or imported by the facility.

Chemical Demilitarization Program: The United States has a legal obligation to destroy its stockpile of unitary chemical weapons under the terms of the Chemical Weapons Convention. As implemented under 50 U.S.C. 1521, the U.S. Department of Defense is tasked with destroying the stockpile; storage and management responsibilities are assigned to the Army Chemical Materials Agency. Originally, there were stockpiles at U.S. Army facilities in Alabama, Arkansas, Colorado, Indiana, Kentucky, Maryland, Oregon, and Utah. Destruction by chemical neutralization has been completed at two locations and is underway by incineration at four sites. Alternative destruction technologies will be used at the remaining two locations. The stockpiles are being destroyed near their storage location; under Public Law 91-121, lethal chemical warfare agents may not be transported to or from any military installation in the United States without a determination that the transport is necessary in the interests of national security.

As part of 50 U.S.C. 1521, the Chemical Stockpile Emergency Preparedness Program (CSEPP) was established in 1988 to enhance emergency preparedness capabilities of the communities adjacent to the chemical stockpile storage facilities. CSEPP, a partnership between the Army Chemical Materials Agency and DHS FEMA, provides funding and technical assistance to State, local, and tribal emergency management agencies in support of a full range of emergency management activities. In its two decades, CSEPP has become a national leader in developing innovative solutions to emergency management challenges with its State and local partners in the fields of alert and notification, automation, communications, coordinated planning, exercises, medical, protective actions, public outreach, and training. Through its publications, workshops, and the CSEPP Portal at **www. cseppportal.net**, the program shares best practices and lessons learned with other programs at all levels of government.

A5.1.3.3 U.S. Department of State Authorities

International Traffic in Arms Regulations: The U.S. Department of State regulates the export of munitions items, which include certain chemical weapons agents and their immediate precursors covered by the CWC, under the International Traffic in Arms Regulations (22 CFR 120 et seq.). Additionally, DOS, as the U.S. National Authority, is responsible for otherwise ensuring U.S. compliance with the CWC.

A5.2 State and Local Authorities

In the absence of overarching Federal regulations in the area, over the past few years, various States and localities have enacted laws or issued regulations under orders imposing security requirements on Chemical Sector infrastructure located or operating within their jurisdiction. Others have legislation pending or are considering proposing legislation at this time. These proposed or existing authorities run the gamut of activities from requiring vulnerability assessments at chemical facilities to banning the transportation of HAZMAT through city limits to increasing the penalty for trespassing at a chemical facility. Each asset owner or operator takes these authorities into consideration when performing the risk management activities at their facilities, as do DHS and the other Federal, State, and local sector security partners.

The following are some of the more significant State or local authorities directed at increasing security at chemical facilities:

State of Maryland, Annotated Code of Maryland, Environment, Sections 7-701 through 7-709: In June 2004, the State of Maryland enacted legislation requiring facilities that handle threshold amounts of HAZMAT to submit to the Maryland Department of the Environment (MDE) by October 1, 2005, and at least every 5 years thereafter, an analysis of the security of the facility. This analysis should include information on potential security threats, vulnerabilities, and consequences. Concurrently, MDE was to develop HAZMAT security standards that require prioritization and periodic analysis of threats, vulnerabilities, and consequences; the development and implementation of security measures commensurate with risk; documentation of security programs, processes, and procedures; training, drills, and guidance for all individuals involved in the sector; a greater communications network and better information sharing; internal audits; and third-party verification. All facilities will be subjected to an audit by MDE or the State Police and be subject to enforced compliance with the standards developed by MDE.

State of New Jersey Domestic Security Preparedness Task Force, Best Practices Standards at Toxic Catastrophe Prevention Act/Discharge Prevention Containment and Countermeasures Chemical Sector Facilities: On November 29, 2005, Acting Governor Richard J. Codey announced a "prescriptive order" issued by the State's Domestic Security Preparedness Task Force. The order applies to a limited number of chemical facilities in the State, and requires them to conduct vulnerability assessments and prepare prevention, preparedness, and response plans. The assessments are to include an evaluation of inherently safer technology. The order also imposes various reporting requirements.

State of New York, State Office of Homeland Security, Article 26, Section 714: On July 20, 2004, the State of New York enacted legislation requiring owners and operators of facilities identified as critical infrastructure within the Chemical Sector to provide all information regarding audits, spill prevention reports, RMPs, and any other report mandated by State and Federal law or regulation to the New York State Office of Homeland Security for review. Based on this information, the Office of Homeland Security must compile a list of facilities that may pose a serious risk based on HAZMAT stored therein, and those facilities must then prepare and submit to the Office of Homeland Security for review a vulnerability assessment of the facility. The Office of Homeland Security must then report the results of its review, including therein security measure recommendations that it believes should be implemented. The New York Department of Environmental Conservation then has discretion to require that an owner or operator of a facility implement the recommendations made by the Office of Homeland Security.

Commonwealth of Pennsylvania, 25 Pa. Code Chapter 211: Storage, Handling, and Use of Explosives: The Commonwealth of Pennsylvania adopted legislation in June 2004 regulating persons using, storing, purchasing, and selling explosives and engaging in blasting activities, with the exception of explosives stored at underground mine sites. The legislation requires procedures, standards, and requirements for licensing, constructing, citing, and maintaining magazines; the sale, purchase, and use of permits; the sale, purchase, use, and storage of records regarding explosives; the transportation of explosives; and the regulation of blasting provisions. The legislation also regulates monitoring procedures and blasting activities near utility sites.

Contra Costa County, California, Industrial Safety Ordinance Code: The ordinance, effective January 15, 1999, is a regulatory requirement for process safety as opposed to security and applies to oil refineries and chemical plants that were required to submit an EPA RMP and are a program Level 3-regulated stationary source as defined by the California Accidental Release Prevention (Cal ARP) Program. These regulated stationary sources are required to consider inherently safer systems when evaluating the recommendations from process hazard analyses for existing processes and to consider inherently safer systems in the development and analysis of mitigation items resulting from a review of new processes and facilities.

Appendix 6: CIKR Partners

Appendix 6A: Additional Federal Departments and Agencies

There are a number of additional Federal departments and agencies that are members of the Chemical GCC because they have responsibilities that affect overall risk management in the Chemical Sector. Some of these Federal entities have regulatory authority with regard to chemicals from either a safety or a security perspective. Other Federal entities provide security-related voluntary programs and activities that benefit Chemical Sector partners. As members of the Chemical GCC, these entities keep sector partners apprised of the latest regulatory issues, voluntary program activities, and those safety issues that are also important to security.

The following is a list of Federal Chemical GCC partners, including a short description of their responsibilities and their association with security in the Chemical Sector.

The Chemical Safety Board (CSB)

CSB is an independent Federal agency charged with investigating industrial chemical accidents, including fires and explosions, toxic gas release, and chemical process safety issues. Congress designed the CSB to be nonregulatory and independent of other agencies so that its investigations might, where appropriate, review the effectiveness of regulations and regulatory enforcement.

The root causes of industrial chemical accidents are usually deficiencies in safety management systems, but can be any factor that would have prevented the accident if that factor had not occurred. Other causes of accidents often involve equipment failure, human error, unforeseen chemical reactions, or other hazards. The agency does not issue fines or citations, but does make recommendations to plants, regulatory agencies such as OSHA and EPA, industry organizations, and labor groups in order to ensure the continued safety of the chemical industry. Many of these safety issues also have implications for chemical security.

U.S. Department of Commerce (DOC)

The historic mission of DOC is to foster, promote, and develop the foreign and domestic commerce of the United States. It has cross-cutting responsibilities in the areas of trade, technology, entrepreneurship, economic development, and environmental stewardship.

The DOC has responsibility for issuing and administering the Export Administration Regulations under laws related to the control of certain exports, reexports, and activities. In this context, DOC controls and licenses certain technologies and commodities, including some chemicals that are included in CFATS Appendix A: Chemicals of Interest List.

Also, the DOC has regulatory authority for implementation of the CWC at domestic industrial facilities. The CWC Implementation Act authorizes DOC to collect information on defined activities involving certain chemicals covered by the CWC, as well as host on-site inspections by the Organization for the Prohibition of Chemical Weapons, the organization responsible for administering and verifying CWC compliance worldwide. DOC's CWC regulations (15 CFR Part 710, et seq.) require facilities involved in CWC-covered activities and chemicals at specific threshold amounts to submit annual declarations and reports and to submit to on-site inspections. The declarations include information on the quantities produced, processed, consumed, exported, and imported by such facilities.

DHS also consults with DOC on the CFATS Appendix A: Chemicals of Interest List in conjunction with CFATS. Experts from DOC are able to provide valuable information on those chemicals that have the potential, if stolen or diverted, to be used as chemical weapons or precursors.

U.S. Department of Defense (DoD)

The mission of the Department of Defense is to provide the military forces needed to deter war and to protect the security of the United States. The Chemical Sector's primary interaction with DoD has been through the analytical capability at the Naval Surface Warfare Center Dahlgren Division (NSWCDD). The NSWCDD conducts research on chemical explosives, propellants, pyrotechnics, and their immediately related components in support of the DoD mission to protect the security of our country. NSWCDD's capabilities include the following:

- Assist the Chemical Sector in identifying chemicals of interest that could be used to create an explosive device;

- Brief the sector on chemical explosives technology; and

- Inform the sector on the latest chemical warfare agent detection methods.

In the future, the Under Secretary of Defense for Policy will provide a representative to the Chemical GCC.

U.S. Department of Energy (DOE)

One of the primary responsibilities of DOE is to promote the Nation's energy security through reliable, clean, and affordable energy. The Chemical Sector relies on the Energy Sector to provide a reliable source of energy in order to produce the chemicals and chemical products that other sectors need to fulfill their functions. In addition, the Chemical Sector relies on the Energy Sector's Oil and Natural Gas (ONG) Subsector to supply chemical manufacturing plants with petrochemicals and natural gas, the primary building blocks for many chemical products. Chemical manufacturing plants are often co-located with petrochemical plants in order to ensure a constant, cost-effective supply of these important chemicals. The need for co-location requires integration and coordination among facilities to reduce the adverse impacts to both sectors during security incidents. The Chemical and Energy Sectors strive to work closely together to ensure that potential impacts are minimized.

U.S. Department of Homeland Security (DHS)

In addition to the DHS entities listed in Section 1.2.1, there are other groups within DHS that impact security in the Chemical Sector. These groups are also members of the GCC and are listed below.

Homeland Infrastructure Threat and Risk Analysis Center (HITRAC) Chemical Representative

HITRAC's mission is to create and disseminate risk-informed analytic products for each CIKR sector. The HITRAC Chemical Representative identifies and assesses threats specific to the Chemical Sector. The representative provides information and briefs for the Unclassified Suspicious Activity Teleconferences and the Biannual Classified Briefings. Additionally, the Chemical Representative has a role in the Strategic Homeland Infrastructure Risk Analysis (SHIRA), a report that assesses the risk to the sector. The responsibilities of the HITRAC chemical representative include the following:

- Evaluate and monitor current threats to the Chemical Sector;

- Maintain situational awareness of the Chemical Sector; and

- Develop long-term strategic assessment of risks by integrating threat information with the unique vulnerabilities and consequences of an attack on the Chemical Sector.

The Office of Intelligence and Analysis (I&A)

The Chemical Team within the Weapons of Mass Destruction and Health Security Branch of I&A is part of the 16-member Intelligence Community and is responsible for producing intelligence on chemical threats to the United States. The I&A Chemical Team is the DHS lead for all-source analysis, production, and coordination of DHS intelligence efforts on all threats to the Homeland involving chemicals. Intelligence analysis and production responsibilities are shared with other members of I&A when the threats involve hostile actors (Homeland Environment Threat Analysis Division); border issues (Border Security Branch); or CIKR such as chemical, water, rail, and so forth (HITRAC/Critical Infrastructure Threat Analysis Division). The responsibilities of I&A include the following:

- Provide all-source analysis of current and future terrorist intent and capabilities to conduct attacks involving chemicals, including chemical warfare agents, toxic industrial chemicals, pesticides, and poisons;
- Represent DHS on national-level working groups and committees related to chemical terrorism; and
- Provide threat information to customers performing risk analysis.

Science and Technology Directorate

S&T is the primary research and development arm of DHS. S&T, in partnership with the private sector, national laboratories, universities, and other government agencies (domestic and foreign), helps push the innovation envelope and drive development and the use of advanced technology in support of homeland security. The majority of the projects of interest to the Chemical Sector are managed by the Chemical and Biological Division of S&T. Their mission is to increase the Nation's preparedness against chemical and biological threats through improved threat awareness and advanced surveillance, detection, and protective countermeasures. The sector is also invited to submit capability gaps through the S&T Integrated Product Team process. A detailed discussion of this process is included in chapter 7.

The Chemical Sector also works closely with the Chemical Security Analysis Center (CSAC) within S&T. DHS established CSAC to provide a scientific basis for the awareness of chemical threats. As such, the primary focus of CSAC is hazardous effects due to chemicals. Located at the Edgewood Area of the Aberdeen Proving Ground in Maryland, CSAC draws upon expertise in chemical defense, chemical agents, and toxic industrial chemicals.

Some responsibilities of S&T and CSAC include the following:

- Enable comprehensive understanding and analyses of biological and chemical threats in the domestic domain;
- Develop the capability for warning, notification, and timely analysis of biological and chemical attacks;
- Provide integration and analysis of chemical threat characterization data; and
- Develop and employ a risk-based approach to address the dangers of toxic chemicals from intentional attacks.

The Office of Health Affairs (OHA)

While serving as the principal agent for all DHS medical and health security matters, OHA also oversees DHS biodefense activities; leads a coordinated national architecture for biological and chemical Weapons of Mass Destruction (WMD) planning and catastrophic incident management; and ensures that DHS employees have an effective occupational health and safety program. Some of the responsibilities of OHA as they relate to the Chemical Sector include the following:

- Oversee the health aspects of contingency planning for all chemical, biological, radiological, and nuclear hazards; and
- Provide incident management and guidance for medical-related security issues during emergencies and catastrophic events.

U.S. Department of Justice (DOJ)

One of the overarching missions of DOJ is to ensure public safety against foreign and domestic threats. The FBI and ATF are two Federal bureaus within DOJ concerned with preventing chemical-based threats to public safety.

The mission of the FBI is to protect the United States against the most dangerous threats facing the Nation. These threats include chemical-based attacks, cyber-based attacks, and high-tech crimes. Given that many common attack methods involve using chemicals in explosive devices, the FBI is actively engaged in outreach efforts in the Chemical Sector. The FBI maintains a dialogue with science departments at academic institutions to promote chemical counterterrorism efforts and awareness through regular university visits and attendance at academic meetings and conferences. Additionally, the FBI conducts counterterrorism awareness and response training at chemical facilities and hosts workshops for chemical industry security managers.

The FBI also developed a Web site specifically for the Chemical Sector called Chemical InfraGard. The FBI's Weapons of Mass Destruction (WMD) Directorate and Cyber Division collaborated on the site's creation to provide information and interactive capabilities aimed at expanding the FBI's outreach efforts in the Chemical Sector.

Among other duties, the ATF is charged with protecting communities from the illegal use and storage of explosives, acts of arson and bombings, and acts of terrorism. The Attorney General has delegated the authority to administer the Federal Explosives Laws to the ATF. The Federal Explosives Laws, 18 U.S.C. Chapter 40, require all persons to store explosive materials in a manner that is in conformity with regulations issued by the Attorney General. The ATF has been working closely with ISCD to ensure that the Secure Handling of Ammonium Nitrate regulations are complementary to the Federal Explosives Laws.

U.S. Department of Labor (DOL)

As part of the DOL, OSHA's role is to promote the safety and health of America's working men and women by setting and enforcing standards; providing education, training, and outreach; establishing partnerships; and encouraging continual process improvement in workplace safety and health. Although safety focused, a number of recognized hazards in the workplace have a direct impact on security-based risk reduction.

OSHA has been given certain responsibilities with regard to chemicals and chemical plant safety through 29 CFR 1910, Occupational Safety and Health Standards.

The sections of the code that are most relevant to the Chemical Sector are Hazardous Waste Operations and Emergency Response (HAZWOPER, 29 CFR 1910.120) and Process Safety Management of Highly Hazardous Chemicals (PSM Standard, 29 CFR 1910.119). The HAZWOPER regulations require the development and implementation of a plan for the entire facility in response to releases of hazardous substances, including evacuation procedures, and training on all sections of the plan. The PSM standard requires facilities using threshold quantities of highly hazardous chemicals to implement an accident prevention program. For example, regulated facilities must assemble Process Safety Information, which includes information on the hazards of chemicals onsite, exposure limits, toxicity, operating limits, and ventilation design. This information is used to conduct a Process Hazard Analysis, which considers what can go wrong and ensures that proper controls are in place to prevent accidental releases. PSM-regulated facilities must also implement additional accident prevention elements, such as using written operating procedures to control evolutions involving highly hazardous chemicals, implementing a mechanical integrity program, investigating incidents involving highly hazardous chemical releases, and other measures.

U.S. Department of State (DOS)

In its mission to create a more secure, democratic, and prosperous world, DOS collaborates with countries, government agencies, nongovernmental organizations, institutions of higher learning, and private sector partners. Several DOS programs are being viewed by Chemical Sector partners in the broader context of reducing the global chemical threat. Important objectives for DOS programs that complement international chemical security include the following:

- Directing international scientists away from using their knowledge of chemicals for unlawful activities, including terrorism, and redirecting them to sustainable civilian employment;

- Fostering a national and regional dialogue focused on improving chemical safety and security in countries and regions where terrorism and the risk of chemical theft and diversion is of the greatest concern; and

- Sponsoring a National Academy of Sciences study on chemical management, including recommendations for improving chemical safety and security in developing nations.

U.S. Department of Transportation (DOT)

DOT is responsible for promoting the safety of the transportation system, through advocacy, regulation, enforcement, grants, and other means. Agencies within DOT with which the Chemical Sector coordinates closely are the Pipeline and Hazardous Materials Safety Administration (PHMSA) and the Federal Railroad Administration (FRA). PHMSA is responsible for protecting people and the environment from the risks inherent in the transportation of hazardous chemicals and materials by pipeline and all other modes of transportation. A major responsibility of FRA is to promulgate and enforce rail safety regulations. The Chemical Sector depends on freight rail to transport a number of important chemicals across the country. FRA-administered regulations that impact freight rail are of special interest to sector partners.

HSPD-7 requires DOT and TSA to collaborate on all matters related to transportation security and transportation infrastructure protection in order to balance protection requirements with the safety, mobility, and economic needs of the Nation. PHMSA, FRA, and other agencies within DOT work closely with TSA to collaborate on voluntary and pilot programs, as well as proposed and implemented security regulations, that cover all three important modes of chemical transport—pipelines, freight rail, and highway.

U.S. Environmental Protection Agency (EPA)

EPA is charged with protecting public health and the environment. One way in which the EPA fulfills its mission is by working with the private sector to ensure that proper safety procedures are in place for hazardous chemicals that can cause adverse health effects or pollute the environment. While EPA programs are designed with regard to safety and the safe handling of chemicals, they may also mitigate the security risks posed by certain hazardous chemicals.

As the SSA for the Water Sector, the EPA is also responsible for source water, drinking water, and wastewater security. These sites are currently excluded from CFATS, yet many of the chemicals used in water purification and sanitation are hazardous and are typically stored in large quantities onsite. Therefore, DHS is particularly interested in working with EPA and the Water Sector to collaborate on CIKR protection and resilience efforts at these sites.

DHS also collaborates with the EPA on certain programs that benefit from the chemical expertise of the EPA. For example, DHS consulted the EPA when developing the proposed rule for CFATS. Additionally, the SSA has collaborated with the EPA and the States to develop a database of sites across the country that must comply with EPA's RMP (which imposes accident prevention requirements similar to OSHA's PSM Standards) and chemical inventory reporting requirements under SARA Title III. The Chemical SSA plans to use this information to identify assets and to use it as a resource for incident management.

The Office of the Director of National Intelligence (ODNI)

The Director of National Intelligence (DNI) serves as the head of the Intelligence Community (IC), overseeing and directing the implementation of the National Intelligence Program and acting as the principal advisor to the President and the National Security Staff,for intelligence matters related to national security. ODNI's goal is to effectively integrate foreign, military, and domestic intelligence in defense of the homeland and in defense of U.S. interests abroad.

With this goal in mind, Congress provided the DNI with a number of authorities and duties, as outlined in the Intelligence Reform and Terrorism Prevention Act of 2004. Some of these duties include the following:

- Ensure that timely and objective national intelligence is provided to the President and the heads of the departments and agencies of the Executive Branch, the Chairman of the Joint Chiefs of Staff and senior military commanders, and Congress;

- Establish objectives and priorities for collection, analysis, production, and dissemination of national intelligence;

- Ensure the maximum availability of and access to intelligence information within the Intelligence Community;

- Oversee coordination of relationships with the intelligence or security services of foreign governments and international organizations;

- Ensure that the most accurate analysis of intelligence is derived from all sources to support national security needs; and

- Develop personnel policies and programs to enhance the capacity for joint operations and to facilitate the staffing of community management functions.

Threat assessment is essential to accurately assess chemical security risk. It is therefore important that the sector has access to the latest intelligence with regard to the threat posed by chemicals, either as key ingredients in explosive devices or as a release hazard.

Appendix 6B: Chemical Sector Coordinating Council Industry Association Members

In the Chemical Sector, there are numerous well-respected industry associations that DHS works with on a regular basis. Relations with industry associations are extremely valuable to DHS because they provide a more manageable number of contact points through which DHS can coordinate activities with a large number of the asset owners and operators in the Chemical Sector. At appropriate times, DHS shares information with, requests information and support from, and provides guidance to the Chemical Sector industry associations. The industry associations that are members of the Chemical Sector Coordinating Council are listed below:

Agricultural Retailers Association (ARA)

ARA is a nonprofit trade association representing the interests of agricultural retailers across the United States on legislative and regulatory issues on Capitol Hill. The agricultural retailer supplies valuable goods and services to our Nation's farmers, including seed, crop protection pesticides, fertilizer, crop scouting, soil testing, custom application of pesticides and fertilizers, and development of comprehensive nutrient management plans. ARA members range in size from family-held businesses to large companies with many outlet stores. Retail facilities are scattered throughout all 50 States and provide important jobs in rural and suburban communities.

American Chemistry Council (ACC)

ACC is a trade association representing many of the leading companies engaged in the business of chemistry. Its 130 member companies employ approximately 523,000 employees, have sales of $332 billion, and operate 2,000 facilities. The Chlorine Chemistry Council (CCC) is a division of ACC that represents the manufacturers and users of chlorine and chlorine-related products. CCC membership includes all leading U.S. chlorine producers.

ACC also sponsors the Chemical Information Technology Council (ChemITC), a self-funded CHEMSTAR Panel under the ACC. ChemITC (**www.chemitc.com**) manages the association's Cyber Security Program.

American Coatings Association

ACA is a nonprofit trade association representing the many diverse segments involved in the coatings industry in the United States—from formulation and testing to manufacture and sales. ACA serves technical, sales, and marketing professionals through education and training, and provides forums for the promotion and advancement of the global coatings industry. The association also provides regulatory, legislative, and market insight services to product distributors and manufacturers of paints, coatings, adhesives, sealants, and caulks, as well as to raw materials suppliers to the industry.

(The ACA was formed from the merger of the National Paint and Coatings Association and the Federation of Societies for Coatings Technology in January 2010.)

American Petroleum Institute (API)

API represents more than 400 members involved in all aspects of petroleum and serves as the primary trade association for the oil and natural gas industry. Members are producers, refiners, suppliers, pipeline operators, and marine transporters, as well as service and supply companies that support all segments of the industry. The association draws on the experience and expertise of members and staff to support a strong and viable oil and natural gas industry.

Chemical Producers and Distributors Association (CPDA)

CPDA is a voluntary, nonprofit membership organization consisting of 86 member companies engaged in the manufacture, formulation, distribution, and sale of approximately $5 billion in crop protection chemicals, fertilizers, and adjuvant and inert ingredients used in food, feed, and fiber crops; the care and maintenance of lawns, gardens, and turf; and in various forestry and vegetation management markets.

The Chlorine Institute

The Chlorine Institute is a trade association of approximately 220 companies and other entities that are committed to the safe and secure production, distribution, and use of chlorine, sodium, and potassium hydroxides, and sodium hypochlorite, and the distribution and use of hydrogen chloride. Chlorine Institute members account for approximately 98 percent of U.S. production of chlorine and the vast majority of repackagers of chlorine into containers for water treatment and other small-quantity uses.

Compressed Gas Association (CGA)

Formed in 1913, CGA has been dedicated to the development and promotion of safety standards and safe practices in the industrial gas industry. CGA's more than 200 member companies worldwide represent all facets of the industry, including manufacturers, distributors, suppliers, and transporters of gases, cryogenic liquids, and related products.

CropLife America (CLA)

CLA represents the developers, manufacturers, formulators, and distributors of plant science solutions for agriculture and pest management in the United States. CLA member companies produce, sell, and distribute virtually all of the crop protection and biotechnology products used by American farmers.

The Fertilizer Institute (TFI)

TFI serves to promote and protect the fertilizer industry, representing the public policy, communications, and statistical needs of producers, importers, wholesalers, and retailers of fertilizer, as well as those companies that provide vital services to the fertilizer industry. Approximately 90 Chemical Sector companies are members of TFI.

Institute of Makers of Explosives (IME)

Founded in 1913, IME is the safety and security association of the commercial explosives industry in the United States and Canada. Membership in IME is available to corporations, partnerships, or firms engaged in the manufacture and distribution of explosive materials for commercial use (excluding fireworks or pyrotechnics) or industrial-grade ammonium nitrate, and firms engaged in the business of supplying or supporting the commercial explosives industry.

International Institute of Ammonia Refrigeration (IIAR)

With more than 1,400 members, IIAR is an international association serving those who use ammonia refrigeration technology. IIAR is known as the authoritative source of information on ammonia refrigeration worldwide. For more than three decades, IIAR members have been sharing their knowledge of and experience with ammonia refrigeration with contractors, equipment manufacturers, and end users.

International Liquid Terminals Association (ILTA)

ILTA is a trade association representing companies and partnerships operating bulk liquid storage terminals in 41 States and 42 countries around the world. Its member companies serve the vital economic purpose of transferring liquid products from one transportation mode to another.

National Association of Chemical Distributors (NACD)

NACD's nearly 240 members purchase chemical products from manufacturers and process, repackage, warehouse, market, and transport these materials to an industrial customer base of approximately 750,000. Chemical distributors serve a wide variety of industries that are critical to the Nation's health and economy, including food and drugs, water treatment, electronics, cosmetics, and paints and coatings. Responsible distribution and customer service are key priorities for NACD members. NACD member companies have established themselves as leaders in health, safety, security, and environmental performance through implementation of the Responsible Distribution ProcessSM (RDP), established in 1991 as a condition of membership in NACD. RDP is a verified, third-party management practice. For additional information, visit NACD's Web site at **http://www.nacd.com**.

The National Petrochemical and Refiners Association (NPRA)

NPRA is a trade association that comprises more than 450 member companies, including virtually all U.S. refiners and petrochemical manufacturers, as well as suppliers. NPRA members supply consumers with a wide variety of products used daily in their homes and business, including gasoline, diesel fuel, home heating oil, jet fuel, lubricants, and the chemicals that serve as building blocks for everything from plastics and clothing to medicine and computers.

Society of Chemical Manufacturers and Affiliates (SOCMA)

SOCMA represents the interests of more than 300 member companies, encompassing every segment of the chemical industry, from small specialty producers to large multinational corporations. SOCMA members are representative of the more than 2,000 batch-processing facilities that produce the most diverse array of chemicals manufactured in the United States, at an estimated annual value of $60 billion. More than 89 percent of SOCMA's members are small businesses.

Appendix 7: State and Major Urban Area Fusion Centers

Many States and larger cities have created State and urban area fusion centers to share information and intelligence within their jurisdictions, as well as with the Federal Government. DHS, through the Office of Intelligence and Analysis, provides personnel with operational and intelligence skills to the fusion centers. This support is tailored to the unique needs of the locality and serves to accomplish the following:

• Help the classified and unclassified information flow;

• Provide expertise;

• Coordinate with local law enforcement and other agencies; and

• Provide local awareness and access.

As of July 2009, there were 72 designated fusion centers around the country with 36 field representatives deployed.

The Homeland Security Data Network (HSDN), which allows the Federal Government to move information and intelligence to the States at the Secret level, is deployed at 27 fusion centers. Through HSDN, fusion center staff can access the National Counterterrorism Center (NCTC) via a classified portal to obtain the most current terrorism-related information.

DHS has deployed intelligence officers to State fusion centers in the following States:

• Arizona	• Louisiana	• Ohio
• California	• Maryland	• Oregon
• Colorado	• Massachusetts	• South Carolina
• Connecticut	• Michigan	• Texas
• District of Columbia	• Minnesota	• Virginia
• Florida	• Missouri	• Washington
• Georgia	• New Jersey	• Wisconsin
• Illinois	• New York	
• Indiana	• North Carolina	

DHS has also deployed support to fusion centers in New York City, Los Angeles, and the Dallas region.

Appendix 8: Private Sector Security Vulnerability Assessment (SVA) Tools and Methodologies

Numerous robust security vulnerability assessment (SVA) methodologies are being used by owners and operators of chemical facilities throughout the Chemical Sector. Some of the more widely used methodologies include the following:

The Agribusiness Security Working Group SVA

In 2003, the Agribusiness Security Working Group, comprising the Agricultural Retailers Association, CropLife America, and the Fertilizer Institute, produced a Web-based tool developed by the Asmark Institute that assists agricultural retailers and terminals in conducting an SVA on their facility and their transportation practices. This program enables retail facilities and terminals to conduct an SVA of their facilities to identify and assess potential security threats, risks, and vulnerabilities, and receive recommendations to improve overall security. The program meets the design criteria of the Center for Chemical Process Safety for conducting SVAs.

The American Chemistry Council

To be a member of the American Chemistry Council (ACC), a company must comply with the Responsible Care® Security Code (RCSC). One of the requirements for compliance is the performance of an SVA under the RCSC. However, instead of developing a new methodology for RCSC compliance, the ACC and other RCSC users opted to employ methodologies already being used throughout the sector. Specifically, to meet RCSC SVA requirements, a facility can use the Vulnerability Assessment Methodology for Chemical Facilities (VAM-CF) developed by Sandia National Laboratories, the Center for Chemical Process Safety (CCPS) SVA developed by the American Institute of Chemical Engineers' Center for Chemical Process Safety, or any other methodology determined by CCPS to exhibit the SVA criteria established by the center. Note that many of these methodologies focus not only on vulnerabilities, but also on the larger issue of risk. It should be noted that the RCSC has been approved by the USCG as an acceptable means of meeting the requirements under MTSA.

In addition to the SVAs recommended as part of the RCSC, the ChemITC Cyber Security Program has developed a guidance document for addressing cybersecurity issues that fall under the RCSC. The guidance is designed to assist companies in improving the security of their information technology and automated ICS.

American Coatings Association

The American Coatings Association amended its Coatings Care® Program to include a Coatings Care Security Code (CCSC), which addresses the critical areas of plant site, transportation, distribution, and cybersecurity with appropriate management practices and guidelines. The CCSC is designed to help companies achieve continuous improvement in security performance using a risk-based approach to identify, assess, and address vulnerabilities in order to prevent or mitigate incidents, enhance training and response capabilities, and maintain and improve relationships with key security partners. Coatings Care® provides coatings manufacturers with accepted and appropriate vulnerability assessment methodology tools to conduct analyses and identify how best to enhance security.

The American Petroleum Institute/National Petrochemical and Refiners Association

The American Petroleum Institute/National Petrochemical and Refiners Association (API/NPRA), as part of its Facility Security Program, developed the API/NPRA SVA methodology. DHS has formally acknowledged that the API/NPRA SVA methodology, published in May 2003, can be used to satisfy DHS requirements, including those of the USCG. The API/NPRA SVA methodology is a comprehensive facility SVA methodology focused primarily on refineries and petrochemical manufacturers.

Center for Chemical Process Safety SVA Methodology

The Center for Chemical Process Safety (CCPS) SVA methodology follows widely accepted SVA methods to evaluate the vulnerability of and, ultimately, the risks faced by chemical facilities with regard to terrorist or other malicious attacks and, based on that assessment, to plan enhanced security where appropriate. Four key vulnerabilities of concern are examined by the CCPS SVA: (1) loss of containment of hazardous chemicals on the plant site leading to health or environmental impact; (2) chemical theft or misuse with the intent to cause severe harm at the facility or offsite; (3) contamination or spoilage of plant products to cause harm; and (4) degradation of the assets, infrastructure, or business function of the facility or company through destructive acts. The CCPS SVA allows for both scenario-based and asset-based vulnerability assessment strategies.

The Chlorine Institute

The Chlorine Institute has developed guidance documents regarding the development of security plans by those who handle chlorine rail tank cars when not under the control of a railroad. The guidance calls for an SVA and contains 36 baseline security actions with implementation recommendations and additional security actions for higher alert levels. Similar programs are in place for those members and their customers who handle chlorine cylinders, ton containers, cargo tanks, and barges.

Institute of Makers of Explosives

The Institute of Makers of Explosives (IME) publishes explosives industry best practices standards. Its Safety Library Publication 27 (SLP-27) covers security in the manufacturing, transportation, storage, and use of commercial explosives. Along with a question-based vulnerability assessment tool and a weighted risk assessment model, SLP-27 also addresses security plans with recommendations geared to threat levels, limiting public disclosure of information on the quantities and the locations of explosives storage and other protected information on a need-to-know basis; relations with local law enforcement and the response community; employee security training, supervising responsibility, and communication with suppliers and customers; and security review with all outside contractors or providers.

Additionally, IMESAFE is a quantitative risk assessment software program for commercial explosives operations. The methodology employed was developed by DOD and has been modified by an expert panel of industry and government advisors to include commercial activities. The DHS threat-level system has been integrated into the software, which increases the probability of an event occurring when applicable.

National Association of Chemical Distributors

The National Association of Chemical Distributors (NACD) revised its Responsible Distribution Process[SM] (RDP) in April 2002 to mandate chemical security measures that address potential vulnerabilities within chemical distribution, including site and transportation security and end-use customers. RDP's security measures also require that SVAs be conducted. Implementation and on-site, third-party verification of RDP, including the security measures, is a condition of membership for companies belonging to NACD. NACD developed the NACD Security Vulnerability Assessment Methodology for Chemical Distribution

Facilities to assist members in meeting their RDP SVA requirements. The methodology is consistent with the Center for Chemical Process Safety SVA criteria when applied to chemical distribution facilities.

Sandia National Laboratories Vulnerability Assessment Methodology for Chemical Facilities (VAM-CF)

The Sandia VAM-CF is a systematic, risk-based method for managing the risk of offsite chemical releases by terrorists. The primary focus of VAM-CF is to address physical site security, including critical unit processes. To a lesser extent, it addresses process control and cybersecurity. VAM-CF consists of seven steps: (1) screening, (2) project definition, (3) planning, (4) site survey, (5) analysis, (6) risk reduction, and (7) the final report. VAM-CF defines risk (R) as a function of the severity of potential consequences (S), the estimated likelihood of attack (LA), and the likelihood of adversary success (LAS). The process is worksheet-driven and designed to be completed by a multidisciplinary team using existing facility data and best judgment.

Society of Chemical Manufacturers and Affiliates Methodology

In November 2002, the Society of Chemical Manufacturers and Affiliates (SOCMA) developed a Chemical Site Security Vulnerability Analysis Methodology and Model (SOCMA SVA) to assist members in assessing vulnerabilities at their facilities. The SOCMA SVA has been recognized by the Center for Chemical Process Safety as meeting its SVA criteria. The SOCMA SVA, a computer-based tool accessible via the SOCMA Web site, has been downloaded more than 1,500 times, is freely available, and is suited to a wide range of facilities in the Chemical Sector. The principal purpose of the SOCMA SVA tool is to assist SOCMA's members in assessing their security vulnerabilities, as required by the ChemStewards® initiative. Generally, however, the SOCMA SVA provides any chemical facility with a mechanism that provides flexibility and efficiency in site vulnerability analysis. The SOCMA SVA can help facilities analyze potential vulnerabilities and consider where resources will be most effective. It is particularly useful for facilities that are not subject to the CFATS regulations and thus are not required to use the CFATS SVA.

Appendix 9: Summary of Cybersecurity Partnership Programs

The Chemical Sector collaborates with NCSD on a number of public-private partnership programs. These programs can be categorized as follows:

- Information sharing;
- Assessments; and
- Exercises.

Listed below is a summary of the current initiatives, including some private sector partnership activities.

A9.1 Information Sharing

- The American Chemistry Council (ACC) ChemITC Cyber Security Program provides an excellent information-sharing forum for ACC member companies. More than 30 member companies are actively engaged in the program, providing funding, as well as 200 volunteers who are working across multiple teams to advance the sector's cybersecurity strategy.

- The Cyber Security Program engages broadly across the Chemical Sector through participation on the Chemical SCC. The council meets six times each year; cybersecurity is an ongoing part of the issues addressed by the council.

- The Chemical Sector addresses cybersecurity issues in a number of forums, including the annual ACC ChemSecure Conference; the 3-day cybersecurity track of the ACC ChemITC annual conference; and the annual Chemical Sector Security Summit, co-sponsored by DHS and the Chemical SCC.

- Representatives from the ACC ChemITC Cyber Security Program work closely with the International Society of Automation in the development of technical papers and standards for industrial automation and control systems security.

- **Roadmap to Secure Control Systems in the Chemical Sector**—Working with the private sector and technology providers, DHS facilitated a robust initiative to define a roadmap to more secure industrial automation and control systems in the Chemical Sector. The document, released in September 2009, will inform the National Coordinating Strategy for Control Systems.

- **Cross-Sector Cybersecurity Working Group (CSCSWG)**—The Chemical Sector regularly participates in this cross-sector working group. There are a number of initiatives that this group is currently pursuing, including the following:

  - **Project 12**—The ACC ChemITC Cyber Security Program contributed to the DHS response to a request for private sector input on Project 12. Project 12, an initiative commissioned by the White House under the Comprehensive National Cybersecurity Initiative (CNCI), published a report detailing the policy and resource requirements for improving the protection of privately owned U.S. critical infrastructure networks. The report detailed how the Federal Government can partner with the private sector to leverage investment in intrusion-protection capabilities and technology, increase awareness about the extent and severity of the cyber threats facing critical infrastructure, enhance real-time cyber situational awareness, and encourage specified levels of intrusion protection for critical information technology infrastructure.

  – **Information Sharing Pilot**—The pilot is a series of monthly conference calls intended to provide a forum for dialogue about security-sensitive, but unclassified, information on potential cyber threats and vulnerabilities. The objective of the pilot is to open the channel of communications between DHS and Chemical Sector partners and encourage information sharing before a significant cyber event occurs.

  – **Metrics Subgroup**—The Chemical Sector has identified sector-level cybersecurity metrics. These metrics will be measured and reported for the first time in 2010, and will continue to be collected and reported on an annual basis.

- **Industrial Control Systems Joint Working Group (ICSJWG)**—Representatives from the Chemical Sector are committed to active involvement in this important NCSD-sponsored cross-sector working group established in March 2009.

- **The United States Computer Emergency Readiness Team (US-CERT)**—The Chemical Sector promotes the use of the sector compartment within US-CERT, which is designed to provide a secure environment for sharing information between DHS and the Chemical Sector.

- **Industrial Control Systems CERT**—Provides recognized cyber incident response and analysis capabilities; addresses the security, threat, and awareness issues unique to control systems; and provides a means to share information across all CIKR sectors.

- **Chemical Sector Monthly Unclassified Suspicious Activity Call**—Cybersecurity professionals from across the Chemical Sector are invited each month to participate in this information-sharing call. These calls include updates from the US-CERT.

- **Sector-Specific Plan**—The ACC ChemITC Cyber Security Program provides cybersecurity input to the overall Chemical Sector-Specific Plan.

- **Sector Annual Report**—The ACC ChemITC Cyber Security Program provides cybersecurity input to the Chemical Sector Annual Report (SAR).

A9.2 Assessments

Cyber Security Evaluation Tool (CSET)—The Chemical Sector continues to increase awareness of the availability of the CSET for use in companies that currently do not use a cybersecurity vulnerability assessment tool.

- **Strategic Homeland Infrastructure Risk Analysis (SHIRA)**—The ACC ChemITC Cyber Security Program participates with the Chemical SSA in the annual development of potential cyber threat scenarios that are deemed to pose the highest threat to the Chemical Sector.

A9.3 National Exercises

- **Cyber Storm II**—The ACC ChemITC Cyber Security Program facilitated the participation of 11 chemical companies in the Cyber Storm II exercise conducted in March 2008. In addition to increased awareness of the cybersecurity issues of the individual companies participating, the exercise revealed the value of a sector-level crisis communications process. An initiative is currently underway in the Chemical Sector to develop a crisis communications capability that includes participation by cybersecurity, physical security, and transportation security professionals.

- **Cyber Storm III**—The Chemical Sector plans to participate in the Cyber Storm III exercise in 2010 to test integration of the new crisis communications process with the National Cyber Incident Response Plan (NCIRP).

A9.4 Infrastructure Security Compliance

The ACC ChemITC Cyber Security Program also provided input to DHS regarding governmental security standards for the Chemical Sector, which has also helped to increase awareness and compliance across the industry.

- **Chemical Facility Anti-Terrorism Standards (CFATS) Risk-Based Performance Standards (RBPS)**—During the development of the regulations, the ACC ChemITC Cyber Security Program made its guidance documents available to DHS to share its knowledge on the use of cyber systems in the chemical industry, as well as the steps that many chemical companies have taken to implement risk-based measures to help enhance the security of these systems. In addition, the Cyber Security Program offered comments on the cyber components of the CFATS-RBPS. The program continues to work with ISCD in communicating the RBPS to the sector and facilitating understanding of how to apply the standards and comply with the cyber components of CFATS.